How To Earn Money Immediately In The Gig Economy Without Having A Traditional Job, The Fastest Way To Attain A Traditional Job Immediately, How To Render Your Resume Attractive To Employers, How To Build A Lucrative Investment Portfolio Without Having Any Money To Invest, How To Build A Lucrative Investment Portfolio That Can Never Lose You Money, How To Retire At A Very Young Age Without Saving Any Money, How To Generate Extreme Wealth Online On Social Media Platforms By Profusely Producing Ample Lucrative Income Generating Assets, The Utmost Best Income Generating Assets To Create For Generating Extreme Wealth Online In The Digital Era, How To Become A Highly Successful Influencer Online On Social Media Platforms, The Plethora Of Assorted Benefits Of Becoming A Successful Influencer Online And Attaining Extreme Fame Leverage, And How To Earn Substantial Money Online So That You Can Afford To Eminently Enrich Every Aspect Of Your Life

By
Dr. Harrison Sachs
Copyright © 2021

# About The Author

Dr. Harrison Sachs is a researcher, author, and epic content creator. He earned a Doctorate of Business Administration in Marketing from Argosy University and an MBA in Marketing from Nova Southeastern University. Throughout his journey as a doctoral student, he maintained an impeccable 4.0 GPA and wrote a mixed methods dissertation appertaining to the influence of YouTube "Let's Play" videos on the purchasing decisions of college students.

Dr. Harrison Sachs has worked as a Digital Marketing Manager and managed to help a company decrease their AdWords marketing costs by 75% while maintaining profitability. He has also created over 100,000 videos for his YouTube channels and has also earned well over 100 million video views from his channels as an aggregate. He continues to live stream and produce vast amounts of new video content on a daily basis to continuously provide the multiverse with unprecedented value. His hobbies encompass organically growing brands, playing chess, playing dodgeball, blogging, writing books, creating enthralling videos, and conducting research.

## Introduction

This essay sheds light on how to earn money immediately in the gig economy without having a traditional job, demystifies the fastest way to attain a traditional job immediately, and explicates how to render your resume attractive to employers. Moreover, how to build a lucrative investment portfolio without having any money to invest is elucidated,, how to build a lucrative investment portfolio that can never lose you money is delineated, and how to retire at a very young age without saving any money is expounded upon. Furthermore, how to generate extreme wealth online on social media platforms by profusely producing ample lucrative income generating assets is elucidated in this essay. Additionally, the utmost best income generating assets to create for generating extreme wealth online in the digital era are identified, how to become a highly successful influencer online on social media platforms is elucidated, and the plethora of assorted benefits of becoming a successful influencer online are revealed in this essay. Moreover, how to attain extreme fame leverage is demystified and how to earn substantial money online so that you afford to eminently enrich every aspect of your life is meticulously expounded upon in this essay. Albeit cumbersome, it is viably possible in the digital era to earn money immediately without having a traditional job. Earning money immediately can entail utilizing gig economy applications in order to find work in the gig economy without having to be interviewed to become an independent contractor in the gig economy. In stark contrast to a traditional job, gig economy workers typically do not need to be interviewed to become independent contractor in the gig economy which ultimately allows them to start working in the gig economy immediately, sometimes even as soon as the next day after they have signed up on a gig economy application to work as an independent contractor on behalf of a gig economy company that furnishes services to customers in the gig economy. Companies that operate in the gig economy and that leverage a workforce of independent contractors to provide services to their customers often have a very quick onboarding process which allows their new fleet of independent contractors to commence providing services to their target market very shortly after they sign up on their gig economy application to become an independent contractor who furnishes services to customers on behalf of the company. Earning money immediately in the gig economy without having a traditional job involves becoming an independent contractor on gig economy platforms that can provide fast payout options to gig economy workers for completing assignments. Not every gig economy platforms offers fast payout options even though a copious amount of them will often have shorter pay periods than traditional employers An exorbitant amount of traditional employers opt to pay their employees on a biweekly basis instead of on a weekly basis which renders it all the more difficult for employees to sustain themselves on a weekly basis. There a copious amount of the gig economy applications which you allow you to become an independent contractor and immediately find work. Someone for instance, who is interested in driving around passengers to their destinations can download riding sharing applications, such as the Lyft application, the Uber application, the Via application, or the Hitch application, and expeditiously become a driver in order to commence earning revenue as a driver in the gig economy. Alternatively, someone for instance, who is interested in delivering food orders to customers can download food delivery applications, such as the DoorDash application, the Grubhub application, the Uber Eats application, the Postmates application, or the Instacart application, and expeditiously become a food delivery in order to commence earning revenue as a food delivery driver in the gig economy. Moreover, someone for instance in providing dog walking services can for instance download dog walking applications, such as the Rover application, the Wag application, the Petbacker application, or the Care application, and expeditiously become a dog walker in order to commence earning revenue as a dog walker in the gig economy. Furthermore, someone for instance in providing technician services can for instance download technician services applications, such as the HelloTech application or the Puls application, and expeditiously commence earning revenue as a technician in the gig economy.

# How To Earn Money Immediately In The Gig Economy Without Having A Traditional Job, The Fastest Way To Attain A Traditional Job Immediately, How To Render Your Resume Attractive To Employers, How To Build A Lucrative Investment Portfolio Without Having Any Money To Invest, How To Build A Lucrative Investment Portfolio That Can Never Lose You Money, How To Retire At A Very Young Age Without Saving Any Money, How To Generate Extreme Wealth Online On Social Media Platforms By Profusely Producing Ample Lucrative Income Generating Assets, The Utmost Best Income Generating Assets To Create For Generating Extreme Wealth Online In The Digital Era, How To Become A Highly Successful Influencer Online On Social Media Platforms, The Plethora Of Assorted Benefits Of Becoming A Successful Influencer Online And Attaining Extreme Fame Leverage, And How To Earn Substantial Money Online So That You Can Afford To Eminently Enrich Every Aspect Of Your Life

Albeit cumbersome, it is viably possible in the digital era to earn money immediately without having a traditional job. Earning money immediately can entail utilizing gig economy applications in order to find work in the gig economy without having to be interviewed to become an independent contractor in the gig economy. In stark contrast to a traditional job, gig economy workers typically do not need to be interviewed to become independent contractor in the gig economy which ultimately allows them to start working in the gig economy immediately, sometimes even as soon as the next day after they have signed up on a gig economy application to work as an independent contractor on behalf of a gig economy company that furnishes services to customers in the gig economy.

Companies that operate in the gig economy and that leverage a workforce of independent contractors to provide services to their customers often have a very quick onboarding process which allows their new fleet of independent contractors to commence providing services to their target market very shortly after they sign up on their gig economy application to become an independent contractor who furnishes services to customers on behalf of the company. Earning money immediately in the gig economy without having a traditional job involves becoming an independent contractor on gig economy platforms that can provide fast payout options to gig economy workers for completing assignments. Not every gig economy platforms offers fast payout options even though a copious amount of them will often have shorter pay periods than traditional employers An exorbitant amount of traditional employers opt to pay their employees on a biweekly basis instead of on a weekly basis which renders it all the more difficult for employees to sustain themselves on a weekly basis.

There a copious amount of the gig economy applications which you allow you to become an independent contractor and immediately find work. Someone for instance, who is interested in driving around passengers to their destinations can download riding sharing applications, such as the Lyft application, the Uber application, the Via application, or the Hitch application, and expeditiously become a driver in order to commence earning revenue as a driver in the gig economy. Alternatively, someone for instance, who is interested in delivering food orders to customers can download food delivery applications, such as the DoorDash application, the Grubhub application, the Uber Eats application, the Postmates application, or the Instacart application, and expeditiously become a food delivery in order to commence earning revenue as a food delivery driver in the gig economy.

Moreover, someone for instance in providing dog walking services can for instance download dog walking applications, such as the Rover application, the Wag application, the Petbacker application, or the Care application, and expeditiously become a dog walker in order to commence earning revenue as a dog walker in the gig economy. Furthermore, someone for instance in providing technician services can for instance download technician services applications, such as the HelloTech application or the Puls application, and expeditiously commence earning revenue as a technician in the gig economy. Additionally, someone who is in completing various tasks, such as assembling furniture or assisting with a move, can for instance download the task rabbit application and expeditiously become a tasker in order to commence earning revenue as a tasker in the gig economy. Moreover, someone who is in working as a tradesman can for instance download the Porch application and can expeditiously start earning revenue as a tradesman in the gig economy.

There are far more gig economy applications available beyond the aforementioned gig economy applications that can help you to find work immediately as an independent contractor without having a traditional job. Furthermore, it is also likely that gig economy applications have a shorter pay period than a biweekly pay period so that their independent contractors can receive their earning more frequently than they otherwise would be able to do so if they worked a traditional job in which they only received revenue payments twice a month. Some gig economy applications can even allow you to receive your payment the same day that you complete gig economy assignments. The advantage of working as an independent contractor without having a traditional job is that you can accept assignments at your own convenience and choose what hours to work which is a stark contrast to a traditional job in which you need to remain adherent to an employer's schedule.

Working as a freelancer on free lancing platforms, such as Fiverr and Upwork, can culminate in taking a while to be able to secure ephemeral freelancing job opportunities, especially as you are in the midst of negotiating contracts with clients. Entering the traditional workforce as an employee can take a substantial amount of time, especially since employers can be unresponsive to your applications. Even if you do manage to receive an interview request from an employer, you may still have to wait ample time to hear back from them to make a hiring decision if they respond to you at all.

Recruiters may also be unresponsive to your applications and may arbitrarily decide not to pass your resume onto an employer. Dealing with recruiters to find you job opportunities can prolong the job search process since they will arbitrarily decide whether or to not pass your resume onto an employer. If you are keen on attaining a traditional job then you should directly apply for the job that you desire to attain and directly contact the hiring manager to ascertain if an interview can be immoderately arranged.

If you are disinterested in working as an independent contractor in the gig economy then you can reach out to temporary employment agencies and ascertain which temporary job opportunities they have available which can potentially lead to long term employment opportunities with the client. The clients of temporary employment agencies may not provide temporary workers with long-term employment opportunities in spite of how productive and competent their temporary workers may be at working the temporary jobs.

If you are disinterested in working as an employer, temporary worker, freelancer, or working in the gig economy then you can earn revenue other ways that do not involve selling your sacrosanct time for revenue. In other words, if you are a property owner for instance, then you rent out a spare room on the Airbnb application to guests or alternatively rent out a spare room on the neighbor application for tenants who can utilize the spare room for storage purposes. If you are a vehicle owner for instance, then you can rent out your vehicle on car rental applications, such as Getaround and Turo. If you have products to sell that you no longer desire to retain then you can sell them via eBay, Amazon, Facebook Marketplace, or Offerup which can be far less time consuming then working a traditional job. In order to generate sales revenue, people can also create a Shopify store and subsequently leverage drop shippers to ship merchandise directly to their customers. There are a copious amount of disparate ways to earn revenue that do not involve working a traditional job for an employer nor incessantly depleting your sacrosanct time to earn revenue. You even have the autonomy to become an entrepreneur and create your own line of work by building lucrative brands and creating income generating assets. In the age of automaton their are a myriad of disparate ways to earn revenue which can even be much higher paying, substantially less time consuming, and far less stressful than working a traditional non-flexible job for an employer on an employer's schedule.

The fastest way to attain a traditional job immediately involves minimizing the time that you spend applying to individual job listings. This ultimately means utilizing quick apply options whenever they are available for you to leverage on job search platforms to be able to apply for jobs. CareerBuilder for instance offer a quick apply to all feature which allows candidates to simultaneously apply to a multitude of jobs that are populated from a job search. Indeed also streamlines the job application process by having an easy apply option for certain jobs that allow candidates to apply for certain jobs in twenty seconds to two minutes. Job candidates also have the autonomy to upload their resumes to job search platforms and render them public so that recruiters can reach out to job candidates.

The fastest way to attain a traditional job immediately is to minimize the amount of time you spend apply to each job listing. You can utilize one resume to apply for every job and list the entirety of your credentials and extensive work history onto the resume so that you do not need to constantly revamp your resume every time that you apply to a disparate job listing. You ideally want to utilize easy apply options to apply to job listings on job search platforms so that the job application process can be streamlined and not involve spending thirty minutes to two hours applying for a single job on an employer's website. By applying to the maximum amount of jobs that you are able to apply for in a short time span, you will become all the more apt to elicit more interview requests then you otherwise would be able to do so if you applied for positions directly on an employer's website. Applying for positions directly on an employer's website can be a very lengthy and time consuming process. If you for instance can apply for over one hundred and sixty jobs in four hours with easy apply options on job search platforms then you will have a much higher likelihood of landing interview requests from employers than if you were to alternatively apply for two to four positions directly on employers' websites. The fastest way to attain a traditional job immediately is to utilize quick apply options on job search platforms and render your resume public on job search platforms so that recruiters can reach out to you which can culminate in more interviews being arranged with employers.

Rendering your resume attractive to employers involves goes beyond the ambit of just listing your ample skills sets, extensive work experience history, educational credentials, and professional certification credentials on your resume. When applying for jobs, employers typically care most about whether or not you have three to ten years of work experience working the job that you are applying to attain. Unfortunately, this creates an impasse for job applications since the so called entry level jobs often require at least three to ten years of work experience working the job that you are applying to attain which ultimately prevents inexperienced job applications for even being considered hireable for that particular job. If a prerequisite to applying for a higher paying job is to have at least three to ten years of work experience working the job that you are applying to attain then your utmost best option for being considered for that job is to work a similar job in a self-employed capacity. By working a job in a self-employed capacity that is similar to the jobs that you are applying for, you render your resume all the more attractive to employers as a result of having accrued applicable work experience.

For instance, someone who is keen on teaching courses at a university, but lacks teaching experience at a university, can increase his chances of being considered for the job if he accrues applicable work experience in a self-employed capacity by creating his own courses and teaching his own courses online on course hosting platforms. Someone who is keen on working as a writer for instance can start their own blog and write their own articles on a daily basis in order to accrue applicable work experience if they are interested in working at a media conglomerate. Someone who is keen on working as a programmer at a software development company can for instance develop their own software applications and release them onto mobile application stores in order to accrue applicable work experience. Someone who is keen on working as a digital marketing manager for e-commerce companies can for instance accrue digital marketing experience by building lucrative brands on social media platforms and marketing their brand content or alternatively by finding clients on freelance platforms to provide digital market services to on a daily basis.. If you can accrue work experience in a self-employed that is germane to the jobs that you are applying for then your resume will be all the more attractive to employers. Rendering your resume all the more attractive to employers is not an easy feat to achieve, especially when you are in the midst of accruing work experience in a self-employed capacity that is germane to the jobs that you applying for. It can ultimately take years to accrue work experience in a self-employed capacity that is germane to the jobs that you applying for. Rendering your resume all the more attractive to employers also entails maximizing your skill sets that are germane to the jobs that you are applying for, maximizing your professional certifications that are relevant to the jobs that you are applying for, and accruing substantial applicable work experience that is pertinent to the jobs that you are applying for.

Rendering your resume all the more attractive to employers also involves doing everything in your purview to stand out from other job applicants. Your resume should be highly organized, ineffably aesthetically appealing, and should be able succinctly list your skill sets, educational credentials, professional certification credentials, and work histories that are germane to the jobs that you are apply for. You can leverage your creativity to render your resume all the more aesthetically appealing and memorable to employers so that your resume is all the more attractive to employers. When submitting a resume to a job listing, you want your resume to metaphorically "put your best foot forward" and serve as a testament to an employer that you are the quintessential candidate for the position based on your skill sets, educational credentials, professional certification credentials, and extensive work histories that are germane to the jobs that you are apply for. Rendering your resume all the more attractive to employers can also involve utilizing creative resume templates to develop a resume that is all the more aesthetically appealing and memorable to employers.

In order to be able to render your resume all the more attractive to employers, it is incumbent that you commence attaining applicable work experience to the jobs that you are applying for, even if that entails having to work in a self-employed capacity to attain relevant work experience to the jobs that you are applying for. Employers are keen on hiring candidates who have accrued at least three to ten years of work experience working the particular job that they are applying to attain. If you have accrued three to ten years of work experience that is germane to the jobs that you are applying for, even if the work experience was attained in a self-employed capacity, then employers will become all the more apt to consider your candidacy for the position. Rendering your resume all the more attractive to employers can amplify your likelihood of landing a job interview in a highly competitive job market in which prospective employees are perceived as a "dime a dozen" by employers.

Albeit cumbersome to achieve, it is viably possible to build a lucrative investment portfolio without having any money to invest. While building a lucrative investment portfolio does not require you to have any money to invest, it does however require you possess a stellar computer, a high speed broadband internet connection, a microphone, and a web camera which you more than likely have already procured. Most people have access to a stellar computer, a high speed broadband internet connection, a microphone, and a web camera since these technologies are needed to allow people to be able to work remotely and communicate with one another remotely. If you do not already own these aforementioned technologies then you will need to procure a a stellar computer, a high speed broadband internet connection, a microphone, and a web camera to be able to build a lucrative investment portfolio does not require you to have any money to invest. In stark contrast to a traditional investment portfolio, in which you are able to rapidly build and expand based on how many investment dollars you have to spend, with an unconventional lucrative investment portfolio does not require you to have any money to invest, you will however be required to spend a substantial amount of time strategically working hard to be able to create the income generating assets that comprise your unconventional lucrative investment portfolio which does not require you to have any money to invest. Income generating assets that you can create can for instance be in the forms of videos, archived live stream broadcasts, songs, podcasts, audio books, eBooks, online courses, software applications, mobile games, and mobile applications. Income generating assets that you can create are intellectual properties that have the latent potential to generate you revenue in perpetuity at any given moment. Unlike traditional income generating assets that costs money to procure, such as stocks with high dividend yields, index funds, mutual funds, annuities, rental properties, or bonds, income generate assets that you can create are intellectual properties that will come at the cost of depleting an exorbitant amount of time strategically working hard to be able to bring to fruition.

In spite of how meritorious your brand content and brand products may be, there is still no guarantee that they will generate you wealth since your target market will determine whether or not your brand content gets consumed and your brand products get procured. When creating videos for instance, it is of salient importance to work strategically hard, compete in niche markets that are not overly saturated with competition, and create video content that is compelling, viral worthy, share worthy, user activity worthy, recommendation algorithm worthy, and memorable so that more people are innately inclined to watch the video, share the video with their friends, comment on the video, and like the video. Your create viral worthy and novel content and products that you bring to fruition should be meritorious and offer unprecedented value to your target market so that you can increase your chances of becoming a dominant market competitor in the niche markets that you compete in. Beyond being monetized, your income generating assets that consist of your viral worthy and novel content and products need to be consistently consumed and/or procured for you to be able to constantly generate income from your income generating assets as an aggregate. Before you commence creating an income generating asset, you should simply ask yourself if you believe that it will be consistently consumed and/or procured in the pending future and desist from in earmarking a substantial amount of your time into creating that income generating asset if you forecast that it will not t will be consistently consumed and/or procured in the pending future by your target market.

Videos for instance become viral videos, because people share them with other people and video recommendation algorithms profusely promote them. Videos with high audience retention rates and high watch times are all the more apt to become viral videos than videos with low audience retention rates and love watch times. Additionally, videos with substantial user activity, such as likes and comments are also more apt to be promoted by the video recommendation algorithms. By creating novel, viral worthy, share worthy, user activity worthy, video recommendation algorithm worthy, and memorable you can expeditiously substantially bolster your brand equity, brand recognition, brand loyalty, and brand growth and rapidly grow an enormous following if your videos build enough traction to become viral videos. Once you have attained extreme fame leverage, you are able to attain extreme wealth which can change every facet of your life even to the extent in which you never have to work another day in your life if you choose not do so due to your lucrative income generating assets being able to always generate enough income to offset your reoccurring expenses. Viral videos are indeed some of the utmost lucrative income generating assets in the world that have the potential to generate revenue in perpetuity as long as they are monetized in someway.

When you build a unconventional lucrative investment portfolio does not require you to have any money to invest, you will be able to avail yourself of multiple streams of income from your income generating assets as an aggregate. By building a unconventional lucrative investment portfolio does not require you to have any money to invest, you can for instance reap sponsorship revenue, affiliate marketing revenue, subscription revenue, donations, advertisement revenue, royalties, and sales revenue If you have been able to cultivate lucrative brands. If you are unable to cultivate lucrative brands and are therefore unable to attain extreme fame leverage then it will undermine your success and earnings potential. By cultivating lucrative brands, you can attain extreme fame leverage and then can subsequently attain extreme wealth. Fortunately, you can still earn sponsorship revenue, affiliate marketing revenue, subscription revenue, donations, advertisement revenue, royalties, and sales revenue even if you have not yet reached the pinnacle of having attained extreme fame leverage. However, your earnings from your income generating assets as an aggregate will be far less than they otherwise would be if you had attained extreme fame leverage.

It is incumbent to an unconventional lucrative investment portfolio does not require you to have any money to invest so that you can make inroads towards having a prosperous, abundant, and auspicious future. If you poor then the only way to pull yourself out of the muck and mire get out of extreme poverty and not live a life fraught with destitution, indigence, and perpetual wage slavery entails being able to generate enough income from your income generating as an aggregate to offset your reoccurring expenses. When cultivating lucrative brands, it is of salient importance to desist from creating copycat brands and instead focus in on becoming reputed as an irreplaceable, one of a kind, unique content creator creator who offers unprecedented value to your target market so that your viral worthy and novel content and products are all the more apt to build traction and/or get procured.

Build a lucrative investment portfolio without having any money to invest not only entails unremittingly working strategically hard on a daily basis for twelve to sixteen hours per day for at least five to fifteen years, creating viral worthy and novel content and products, growing lucrative brands, and compete in niche markets that are not overly saturated with competition, but also entails doing everything in your purview to minimize your reoccurring expenses so that you can have the requisite time to be able to create income generating assets without having to sell your sacrosanct time to an employer for a pittance of a non-subsistence wage to generate revenue. If you need to work a part-time job for an employer in the interim before you income generating assets as an aggregate generate enough income to offset your reoccurring expenses then it will significantly prolonged to build a lucrative investment portfolio without having any money to invest since you cannot create as many income generating per year as you otherwise would have been able to if you were not working a highly time consuming, dead end, minimum wage, dispiriting, unfulfilling, undesirable, harrowing, brutally wretched job that does not even pay you anything close to a subsistence wage for attaining the utmost lowest level basic needs that are relegated to the utmost lowest level tier on Mallow's Hierarchy of needs pyramid.

Most companies will never pay their employees anything even close to a subsistence wage. The overarching goal of most companies is to maximize their profits and maximize the wealth of their shareholders and not prioritize the well-being of their employees, even though the employees are the backbone of companies who allow companies to operate profitably.

Most Companies view their employees as exploitable, expendable, capital live utilized for profiteering purposes by employers, but also deem their employees to be labor cost liabilities as a labor cost expense to be minimized. The overarching goal of most companies to maximize their profits and wealth of their shareholders. This goal of maximizing their profits and wealth of their shareholders is diametrically opposed to satisfying the needs of their employees. Based on their coveted desire to always improve their performance outcomes, it will often come at the cost of the employees well-being.

If you do not have time to create income generating assets nor build lucrative brands then this can leave you perpetually entrapped in a life fraught wage slavery, destitution, indigence, and poverty since the only way to get out of poverty is to have the revenues generated from your income generating assets offset your reoccurring expenses. If you cannot afford to buy income generating assets nor do not have the requisite time to be able create income generating assets then this can leave you entrapped in a life fraught wage slavery, destitution, indigence, and poverty, especially as the cost of living continues to amplify while the standard of living continues to plunge. Selling your sacrosanct time for a pittance of non-subsistence wage creates a recipe for a life fraught with insurmountable struggles, enormous debts, indigence, destitution, extreme poverty, and poor health.

Employees who work real private sector jobs based on voluntary demand live credit card to credit card, are insurmountably indebted, and do not even have enough money to be able to attain the utmost lowest level basic needs on Maslow's hierarchy of needs pyramid in spite of working an exorbitant amount of hours at their dead end, minimum wage, dispiriting, unfulfilling, undesirable, harrowing, distressful, brutally wretched jobs. Working dead end, minimum wage, dispiriting, unfulfilling, undesirable, harrowing, distressful, debilitating, brutally wretched jobs is a highly time consuming consuming, highly stress inducing, and ineffably agonizing experience that renders someone all the more prone to experiencing the brunt of chronic burnout, chronic fatigue, and chronic stress.

' When company's enact pay cuts, set even loftier unrealistic employee expectations that cannot be met, require employees to perform more responsibilities outside the scope of their job, require employees to work off the clock, and require employees to cover other people's shifts at the last minute without giving any advance notice, then this will allow companies to operate more profitably even though it will often adversely impact the employee's well-being. Most companies do not care an iota about the well-being of their employees since they staunchly believe that maximizing the well-being of their employees is not conducive to maximizing their profits nor wealth of their shareholders.

Companies that do not care a modicum about the well-being of their employees are more prone to experiencing higher employee attribution rates and incurring higher employee turnover costs. Employees make tremendous sacrifices to satisfy their ever growing employer's needs at the cost of their time, well-being, health, and happiness, and employers are often unwilling to be understanding nor accommodating of their employee's needs.

In spite of all the tremendous sacrifices that employers make to satisfy their ever growing employer's needs, most employees who work real private sector jobs based voluntary demand work highly time consuming, debilitating, dead end, minimum wage, dispiriting, unfulfilling, undesirable, harrowing, distressful, brutally wretched jobs that drain almost all their sacrosanct time and that do not pay anything close to 1/4 of a subsistence wage for affording housing. It is not uncommon for the average employee who works a real private sector jobs based on voluntary demand to have at least $80,000 of debt as their negative net worth when they pass away since the cost of living is so egregiously high and the standard of living is so egregiously low.      Working as a wage slave provides a an egregiously low standard of living since working highly time consuming, debilitating, dead end, minimum wage, dispiriting, unfulfilling, undesirable, harrowing, distressful, brutally wretched jobs that drain almost all of their sacrosanct time and that do not pay anything close to 1/4 of a subsistence wage for affording housing not only drains almost all of your sacrosanct time, does not allow you to afford to attain the utmost basic needs that are relegated to the utmost lowest level basic needs on Maslow's hierarchy of needs pyramid, induces chronic burnout and chronic fatigue, but also deplete your sacrosanct time needed to create income generating assets and build lucrative brands.

In order to pull yourself out of the muck and mire and overcome the seemingly insurmountable challenge of escaping living a life fraught with extreme poverty, destitution, indigence, insurmountable debt, and perpetual wage slavery it is of eminent importance to you strategically work hard to cultivate lucrative brands and create income generating assets so that you can offset your reoccurring expenses which will allow you to liberate your time and have more time to be able to further build your unconventional lucrative investment portfolio that consists of your income generated that you brought to fruition..

The cost of building a lucrative investment portfolio can drain at least 21,900 - 87,600 of your sacrosanct time in which you need to work strategically hard to cultivate lucrative brands and create viral worthy and novel content and products. The cost of building a lucrative investment portfolio without having any money to invest not only entails unremittingly working strategically hard on a daily basis for twelve to sixteen hours per day for at least five to fifteen years, creating viral worthy and novel content and products, growing lucrative brands, and compete in niche markets that are not overly saturated with competition, but also entails doing everything in your purview to minimize your reoccurring expenses so that you can have the requisite time to be able to create income generating assets without having to sell your sacrosanct time to an employer for a pittance of a non-subsistence wage to generate revenue.

As a content creator, it is of eminent importance that you create income generating assets that are apt to build traction overtime, be recommended by the algorithms, draw forth user activity, and be shared by others so that they are all the more apt to become viral. It is imperative to do everything in your purview to win over the lifetime values of customers and cultivate lucrative brands which is why you should aim to work unremittingly strategically hard for at least twelve to fourteen hours per day to create viral worthy and novel content and products that provide unprecedented value to your target market in the niche market that you compete in. Building a lucrative investment portfolio without having any money to invest is no easy feat and is not for the faint of heart even though it is is achievable.

The amount of revenue individuals can generate from a young age in the digital without needlessly hemorrhaging their time is unprecedented. For example, it was reported that "Ryan, a-then-7 year old content creator, made $11 million from his YouTube channel, coming in at number 8 on Forbes' 2017 list. His YouTube channel has attracted a huge following of parents and children who watch Ryan test out new toys and share his thoughts on them" (O'Kane, 2018). He is in fact so successful at creating a lucrative brand around his passion that he has earned more revenue in one month at the tender age of 7 than the average adult will ever earn working multiple jobs throughout the entirely of their lifetime. When children begin to work from a young age on developing brands around their passions and interests, the outcomes can render them poised for unprecedented success as adults, especially if they already have amassed ample work experience and already built lucrative brands during their childhood years which they can further grow amid their adulthood years.

Attaining extreme fame leverage so that your income generating assets can be profusely consumed by your target market starts by becoming an influencer and enticingly marketing your content in order to build brand equity, brand loyalty, and brand recognition. You ideally want your brand's social media accounts to become the preferred social media channels for your niche content genre. By building your brand equity and your following on your social media channels, you will eventually be able to charge any extremely exorbitant price you see fit just to sell a single product placement on your brand's social media account, such as by charging $1,000,000 for a single product placement in the form of an Instagram photo just like Kylie Jenner. Brands can vindicate paying $1,000,000 for a single product placement if your social media accounts have enough followers apart of their target market which is all the reason why it is more incumbent than ever before to attain extreme fame leverage so that you can subsequently attain extreme fame wealth by having your brand become the utmost preferred and popular social channel for your niche content genre.

On your journey to becoming highly successful, it is of eminent importance that you focus on creating viral worthy and novel content and products. Generating extreme wealth online on social media platforms for instance can entail frequently creating ample lucrative income generating assets, such as viral videos, popular automated online courses, popular books, popular mobile applications, popular mobile games, popular software applications, popular podcasts, and viral songs.

If you are strategically working hard, but are not creating viral worthy content nor products then it is unlikely that you will become profoundly successful. If you are strategically working hard, but are not ushering in novel content nor products into the niche markets that you compete in and are instead focused on growing a copycat brand which creates similar content and products to other market competitors then it is unlikely that you will become profoundly successful. If you are strategically working hard, but are competing in an overly saturated market then it is unlikely that you will become profoundly successful, especially since it becomes all the more cumbersome for a brand to build traction when it is overshadowed by long established brands in hyper competitive markets.

Becoming profoundly successful will not only require you to unremittingly work strategically hard on a daily basis, constantly create more lucrative income generating assets, and incessantly create viral worthy and novel content and products, but will also require you to become a dominant market competitor in the niche markets that you compete in. Moreover, you will also need to attain extreme fame leverage and extreme wealth to be able to have a chance of achieving multimillionaire status in your lifetime. In spite of your utmost best efforts and the merits of your brand content and products, there is still no guarantee that you will be able to become a multimillionaire even if you earmark at least hundreds of thousands of hours of strategic hard work on your end as an entrepreneur and content creator into this pursuit of achieving multimillionaire status in your lifetime.

Successfully changing your life is simple and entails strategically working hard, embracing an abundance mindset, focusing in on optimizing your health, and taking the requisite measures to draw forth the utmost best version of yourself. Successfully changing your life will require you to not only learn the necessary measures to implement in order to be able to move your life in forward moving trajectory, but will also require you to have the audacity to implement major changes in your life.

Most people are deterred from building an unconventional lucrative investment portfolio does not require you to have any money to invest since they are unwilling to invest an exorbitant amount of time strategically working hard to be able to manifest these income generating assets into reality. Not everyone can handle being a content creator, live streamer, blogger, author, musician, global educator, podcast host, nor developer. On the other hand, in stark contrast to building a traditional lucrative investment portfolio that is expensive to be able to build and expand and easily achievable if you are wealthy, building an unconventional lucrative investment portfolio does not require you to have any money to invest can be ineffably cumbersome and requires years of unremittingly working strategically hard for tens of thousands of hours to be able to have a modicum of a chance to expeditiously build unconventional lucrative investment portfolio

Much to the relief of the individual, it is possible to build an unconventional lucrative investment portfolio that allows you to never lose money. In the event that your brands do not build traction and your income generating assets that you created are not generating revenue from your brand content and products not being consumed and/or procured, you will not lose money, but rather will just have squander the time you invested income creating these income generating assets. However, if your income generating assets that you created are not generating revenue from your brand content and products at this juncture there is still a possibility that they can be consumed and/or procured in the pending future, especially if they are viral worthy and novel content and products that offer unprecedented value to your target market in the niche markets that you compete in. It is enigmatic as to whether or not your content and products will build traction, be promoted by the recommendations algorithms, be shared by others, and go viral. Your target market will decide whether or not you are successful and will have bearing on whether or not your unconventional lucrative investment portfolio comprised of the income generating assets that you created generates wealth. While it is possible to build an unconventional lucrative investment portfolio that allows you to never lose money, it is also possible to build an unconventional investment portfolio comprised of intellectual properties that you created which never generates substantial revenue. When you create an income generating asset it is enigmatic how much revenue it will generate in the pending future. On the other hand, with a traditional investment portfolio that is comprised of income generating assets that you buy, such as index funds, bonds, and stocks with high dividend yields, it is more predictable how much revenue you can expect to generate per year from coupon payments and dividend payments.

Albeit ineffably cumbersome, it is possible to retire at a very young age without saving any money. You do not need to embrace minimalism nor even invest the revenue generated from your income generating assets income into buying more lucrative income generating assets to be able to retire at a young age even though doing the aforementioned could allow you to retire at a younger age then you otherwise would be able to do so if never embraced minimalism nor ever bought an income generating asset to compound your wealth. In other words, retiring at a young age without ever saving money simply entails being able to generate enough wealth from your income generating assets as an aggregate to offset your reoccurring expenses. Since you can create income generating assets you do not need to buy income generating assets to able to generate the wealth from your income generating assets as an aggregate that is necessary to offset your reoccurring expenses. Income generating assets that you can create can for instance be in the forms of videos, archived live stream broadcasts, songs, podcasts, audio books, eBooks, online courses, software applications, mobile games, and mobile applications.

Whether or not you will be able to retire at a very young age is predicated upon whether or not your income generating assets as an aggregate will be able to generate enough wealth to offset your reoccurring expenses. If you have attained extreme fame leverage, have established lucrative brands, have attained market dominance in the niche markets that you compete in, and have viral content and products then it is highly likely that you will be able to retire at a young age without saving any money. This is because, in this context of having attained extreme fame leverage, having established lucrative brands, having attained market dominance in the niche markets that you compete in, and having viral content and products, you will be apt to attain extreme wealth which will presumably allow your income generating assets as an aggregate to generate enough wealth to offset your reoccurring expenses. Fortunately, if you strategically work hard for at least twelve to sixteen years per day for at least five to fifteen years, cultivate lucrative brands, create a copious amount of viral worthy and novel content and products that offer unprecedented value to your target market in the niche markets that you compete in, attain market dominance in the niche markets that you compete in, attain extreme fame leverage, and create a copious amount of income generating then you will become all the more poised to attain extreme wealth and be able to retire at a young age without having any money.

It is possible to retire at a very young age even if you desist from saving any money. It is for instance estimated that Ryan from Ryan's World for instance, who started creating income generating assets and cultivate a lucrative brand at a young age earned over $29,500,000 in 2020 at the tender age of 9 years old. "Ryan began making YouTube videos in 2015 when he was just four-years-old. 'Ryan's World' remains the most popular with 27.7 million subscribers. The channel has grown from toy reviews to more informative content over the years. On the channel, Ryan today shares a mix of fun and educational videos, such as do it yourself science experiments and clips of him taking part in various challenges". As of February 2021, The Ryan's World YouTube channel has earned over 28,400,000 subscribers and over 45,185,000,000 and is slated to continue to grow. Ryan has the autonomy to be able to easily retire if so chooses to do. When you are able to cultivate lucrative brands at a young age, create a copious amount of viral worthy and novel content and products that offer unprecedented value to your target market in the niche markets that you compete in, attain market dominance in the niche markets that you compete in, attain extreme fame leverage, and create a copious amount of income generating then you will become all the more poised to attain extreme wealth and be able to retire at a young age without saving any money. Accomplishing this feat of being able to retire at a young age without saving any money can cost you a substantial amount of your sacrosanct time that you will need to prudently earmark into creating ample lucrative income generating assets and cultivating lucrative brands at a young age. Being able to render at a young age without saving any money is an accomplishment that most people believe does not warrant the cost which is an upfront time investment in which you strategically work hard on a daily basis for long hours to cultivate lucrative brands and create a copious amount of viral worthy and novel content and products that offer unprecedented value to your target market in the niche markets that you compete in order to attain market dominance in the niche markets that you compete in and attain extreme fame leverage so that you can subsequently generate extreme wealth and be able to retire at a young age without saving any money if your income generating assets as an aggregate are able to offset your reoccurring expenses. Your target market will determine whether or not you will reach the lofty pinnacle of success that allows you to retire at a young age without saving any money. Your target market determines whether or not your content and products whether or not they go viral and are able to generate extreme wealth,

    Albeit challenging, it is possible to pull yourself out of the muck and mire as an adult and escape the financial perils of living a life fraught with wage slavery in which you become more indebted every year from your dead end, minimum wage, dispiriting, unfulfilling, undesirable, harrowing, distressful, brutally wretched wretched job providing you with a pittance of a wage that loses purchasing power every year due to incessant inflation rate increases. Those who able to successfully parlay their talents into generating extreme wealth online also understand that the formula for generation wealth.

Contrary to what you might expect, the formula for generating wealth is simple and can be utilized to predict the future profitability outlook of a business. Succinctly stated, the formula for generating wealth entails the following: scalability + magnitude + marketing effectiveness = wealth. This formula can serve as an indicator to not only help predict the future profitability outlook of an online business, but also its longevity. In other words, if an online business is egregiously lacking in one of these aforementioned facets, such as scalability, magnitude, or marketing effectiveness, its future will more than likely be precarious and fraught with calamitous issues, especially as competition in their niche market continue to be on the rise.

Generating extreme wealth online online on social media platforms will require you to constantly strategically work hard seven days per week in order to build your brand's content reservoir vy profusely producing ample lucrative income generating assets. You will also have to profusely create unique, engrossing content that adds unprecedented value to your niche content genre if you want to have a modicum of chance to generate extreme wealth.

Moreover, if you are a content creator, then you will also be afforded the opportunity to create video content and upload them onto video hosting platforms, such as YouTube or DailyMotion. Additionally, you can even broadcast your live video content via live stream platforms, such as Twitch and Smashcast.TV. Content creators and live streamers earn donations, advertisement revenue, subscription revenue, royalties, affiliate marketing revenue, and sponsorship revenue. Viewers donate to content creators via platforms such as, Patreon, Muxy, and Streamlabs, and also buy their brand merchandise via the content creator's online store, such as their Teespring Store.

If you are a writer, you can publish your articles onto blogging platforms, such as Blogger or Medium. Moreover, if you are an author then you can publish your eBooks via Amazon Kindle Direct Publishing and can also publish your audio books onto Audible for the prospect of earning royalties from book sales.

If you are a developer then you can develop your own mobile applications and games. These mobile applications and games can be published onto platforms, such as Google Play Store, the Apple Store, and the Amazon Appstore, and can allow to reap royalty payments from product sales.

If you are a musician then you can publish your own songs to music streaming platforms, such as Spotify and Pandora, in order to reap royalty payments from your own songs being played on these music streaming services. Buying a computer and internet connection will afford you the opportunity to have the chance to become an influencer, grow your brands, work remotely, and attain extreme fame leverage.

Maximizing your earnings potential is viably possible by attaining extreme fame leverage and cultivating highly lucrative brands on social media platforms. While it can take tens of thousands of hours of strategically and unremitting working hard to grow your brands to the point of profitability, the grim reality of the situation is that these opportunities to create income generating assets, build brands online, work remotely, and become an online influencer are not possible without a computer nor internet connect. In other words, buying a high quality computer and paying for broadband internet access may turn out to be the utmost lucrative long term investment you ever made in your life if you are able to attain extreme fame leverage by growing behemoth of online brands on social media platforms as an influencer of your niche area of expertise. An influencer who has attained extreme fame leverage can generate far more revenue in a single day than the average person will earn working multiple run of the mill jobs throughout the entirety of their life.

Generating extreme wealth online on social media platforms entails profusely producing ample lucrative income generating assets, such as viral videos, popular automated online courses, popular books, popular mobile applications, popular mobile games, and viral songs. Income generating assets can be in the forms of videos, archived live stream broadcasts, songs, podcasts, audio books, eBooks, physical books printed on demand, online courses, software applications, mobile games, and mobile applications. These income generating assets allow you to generate wealth at any time and do not cap your earnings potential based on a pittance of an infinitesimal, minimum wage from an employer that does not even provide a sustenance wage for afford housing. By attaining extreme fame leverage on social media platforms, you will be able to generate extreme wealth from sponsorship revenue, affiliate marketing revenue, subscription revenue, donations, advertisement revenue, royalties, and sales revenue. Once you have attained fame leverage on social media platforms as an influencer and content creator in your niche area of expertise, such as fashion or cooking, your audience will more apt to consume anything you churn out and will also be more inclined to buy any products that you recommend purchasing.

Attaining extreme fame leverage so that your income generating assets can be profusely consumed by your target market starts by becoming an influencer and enticingly marketing your content in order to build brand equity, brand loyalty, and brand recognition. You ideally want your brand's social media accounts to become the preferred social media channels for your niche content genre. By building your brand equity and your following on your social media channels, you will eventually be able to charge any extremely exorbitant price you see fit just to sell a single product placement on your brand's social media account, such as by charging $1,000,000 for a single product placement in the form of an Instagram photo just like Kylie Jenner. Brands can vindicate paying $1,000,000 for a single product placement if your social media accounts have enough followers apart of their target market which is all the reason why it is more incumbent than ever before to attain extreme fame leverage so that you can subsequently attain extreme fame wealth by having your brand become the utmost preferred and popular social channel for your niche content genre.

The more enthralling content you create, the higher likelihood you will have of generating extreme wealth online. This is because captivating content can go viral at any given time and the odds of you attaining profound success and fame leverage on social media platforms amplify as you produce more desirable content subsumed under your niche content genre. Creating a copious amount of income generating assets and brand content is of paramount importance for content creators and influencers keen on having a chance of generating extreme wealth online.

The utmost best income generating assets to create for generating extreme wealth online in the digital era encompass viral videos, popular digital courses, popular ebooks, popular mobile applications, popular mobile games, and viral songs since they have allowed a copious amount of people to multimillionaires. The formula for generating wealth can be applied to understand how these products have rendered individual's multimillionaires.

These digital products have limitless scalability since they can incessantly be globally, digitally distributed across multiple digital distribution platforms which affords you the opportunity of being able to generate wealth at any given from anyone apart of your target market. These digital products can also have profound magnitude since you can charge any price you see fit for customers to pay to purchase your digital products. Moreover, as per viral videos, you can even leverage the descriptions of viral videos as advertisement real estate for selling product placements. Some content creators, influencers, and global educators even charge their students over $2000 just to enroll in one of their online courses.

The marketing effectiveness of your social media marketing efforts and enticing pay-per-click digital market campaigns to market your digital products will have tremendous bearing on your ability to generate extreme wealth. Pay-per-click digital market campaigns will allow you to instantly reach millions of new customers who may be inclined to consume your brand content or buy your products. An investment in building your social media followings through Pay-per-click digital market campaigns that does not culminate in leading to product sales may not be a complete squanderance of marketing dollars. This is because, it may result in providing you with more fame leverage and brand equity as you build your follows which can be beneficial for selling future products placements at loftier premium prices to companies. Companies will prefer to buy product placements from renowned influencers who have the ability to reach more customers subsumed under their target market than influencers who have less sizeable followings.

If you can establish massive followings across multiple social media channels than you can more easily generate extreme wealth even if you decide to minimize the amount of content you create once you have garnered an unmistakable reputation for not only having extreme fame leverage, but for also be the leading influencer in your niche area of expertise.

Attaining extreme fame leverage is a precursor for being able to attain extreme wealth since you will need to maximize the viewership and amount of attention directed onto your brand content if you want to have a chance of being able to stimulate product sales and generate extreme wealth. Content creators and influencers who do not have their brand contented viewed nor products well known will struggle to generate revenue since the customer's attention needs to directed onto your brand content and digital products to have a chance of generating revenue. Companies, such as Amazon and AT&T, will even deplete multibillion marketing budgets every year just to ensure that customer attention will be directed onto their products and/or service. If you attain extreme fame leverage as a renowned influencer and prolific content creator then attaining extreme wealth through your brand content being consumed and your products being sold becomes a much easier and more seamless undertaking.

Even though becoming a highly successful influencer on social media platforms in the digital era may seem like a daunting, lifelong task as hyper competition on social media platforms continues to grow to an unprecedented height, it is more viable than anytime in history. In spite of this, the tried and true methodology for attaining a world renowned reputation online as an influencer continues to work for individuals that are eager to diligently follow a series of incremental steps to transform themselves into influencers of their respective niches. In other words, the process of becoming an illustrious influencer can be broken down into a myriad of steps that first commences with finding a niche sub-genre to create content about for the world to feast its eyes on.

As per the first step, you should ideally create content subsumed under a niche sub-genre that you are passionate about since you will be creating content for years as an influencer and do not want your career to become a harrowing, dreadful, agonizing, and debilitating undertaking. You should also focus on creating content for a niche sub-genre that is not oversaturated with hyper competition so that growing your brand as an influencer is a less overwhelming and more seamless process.

As per the second step, once you have selected the niche sub-genre your content will be subsumed under, you will need to strategically plan how your content will be disparate from competitor videos. You need to devise your content strategy and map out how you will offer unprecedented value to your target market. "Part of developing an effective content strategy is giving your audience the right balance of informative content and personal content. Remember, one reason why people trust influencers is due to their relatability. Influencers are known for being able to provide valuable content to their audience. That also includes sharing content written by others that they believe their followers will find useful. More important, sharing content published by other influencers in your niche will help you slowly get their attention. As a result, it will be much easier to reach out to them and ask them to do the same for you later on" (Payne, n.d.).

In terms of content strategizing, there are a copious amount of ways in which an influencer can provide value as a prolific content creator that goes far beyond sharing the enthralling content of others across social media platforms. For instance, if you have a YouTube channel in which you create videos appertaining superhero comic books, it is not enough just to review comic books, discuss comic book news, and predict how events will unfold in upcoming Marvel comics or DC Comics storylines. You may also need to create your own comic book theory videos, provide videos that share the stories of alternative plots you devised for the comic books, and you may need to create biography videos of comic book characters that provides insights appertaining to the prodigious backgrounds of particular characters. Moreover, you can also reenact comic book scene with action figures embroiling in combat through the usage of stop motion capture. Moreover, you can also create funny superhero prank videos in public and can also provide insights for how novice artists can draw their favorite comic book characters.

Ideas for video content creation of a niche sub-genre are plentiful and endless. You will need to be highly creative, innovative, inventive, and constantly think outside the parameters of the metaphorical box if you want to become an influencer since you will need to attain robust brand growth to become an influencer worthy of receiving endorsement deals. Creating content similar to competitors, especially in highly oversaturated user-generated content markets is a recipe for unalloyed failure.

It is imperative that you narrow down your content focus so that it is unequivocally clear to your viewers what your target market can expect from your channels. You do not want to draw forth flusterations from your followers by it being unclear what your brand represents and is oriented around nor do you want to succumb to loosing followers by creating content from multiple disparate genres that are completely unrelated. "Focusing on one specific theme for each of your social media channels allows you to give your followers a more holistic picture of who you are, what you do, and what you stand for. That way, you're able to publish more diverse content while still keeping your profiles very sleek and cohesive. More important, it helps you categorize the different types of content you publish. That way, your followers know which social media channel they will find the content they need from you" (Payne, n.d.).

As per the third step, once you have select your niche sub-genre of content and strategically planned how you will eminently distinguish your video content from competitors' video content, you will then need to create social media handles and subsequently strategically choose which social media platforms that you would like to compete on and market your content onto. As mentioned prior, some popular social media platform encompass YouTube, Instagram, FaceBook, Twitch, Twitter, Tumblr, LinkedIn, and Pinterest. You should prioritize focusing on utilizing one or two of the utmost popular social media platforms for hosting your content onto which receives the greatest amount of traffic from your target market, such as YouTube if you are also video content creator or Instagram if you are mostly photo-based content creator.

As previously mentioned, the other social media platforms that you do not directly host your content onto, such as Twitter and FaceBook, will simply be leveraged by you as inbound marketing mediums for the purposes of profusely disseminating your content to maximize your reach online. Once viewers stumble upon your content through these other social media channels that your content has been shared onto through content marketing messages, they will be able to redirected to the original source of your content. Once they have migrated to the hub channel that your content is hosted onto, they will have the option to subscribe to your channel if they are interested in watching your upcoming content you plan to churn out in the pending future.

As previously punctuated, just like the independent video game developer, the influencer an also capitalize on the utilizing IFTTT to create recipes to automate the dissemination of his social media marketing content. This is because, IFTTT is able to automatically disseminate the influencer's content, such as their YouTube video content, to a myriad of platforms simultaneously, such as Twitter, Pinterest, Tumblr, Blogger, and others social media outlets. The influencer can set the IFTTT recipes to trigger upon the condition of new videos being uploaded to YouTube. By automating content marketing practices and social media marketing practices by leveraging IFTTT recipes, influencer can focus on spending far time producing content and less time marketing content.

As per the fourth step, once you have established your IFTTT recipes, social media accounts, and content strategy for how you will add profound uniqueness to the body of user-generated content of your sub-genre, you will need to commence creating your social media content consistently which move more then likely be video content since videos are the preferred media. You will need to render your content compelling, unique, and worthy of sharing. You will need to consistently and profusely create ample enticing content to increase the likelihood of your content building traction and going to viral.

For influencers, it is highly advantageous to create as many videos as possible when cultivating a brand. Videos are far more likely to be viewed and shared than articles and therefore have a far likelihood of going viral than other types of user-generated content.

Viral videos for instance can substantially help a brand bolster profitability, brand growth, brand recognition, brand loyalty, and brand equity since the impact they have on growing a brand to the next level is eminently profound. Since it is arduous for a video to become rendered a viral video in a hyper competitive video market, it is pivotal that the content creators focus on creating as many videos as possible that have the potential to go viral. These videos should embrace the key elements of a viral video to significantly increase their likelihoods of going viral.

Video videos are often relatable, short, personable, funny, and authentic. Moreover, viral videos typically have ample back links that direct viewers to them and viral videos utilize catchy titles, optimal keywords as tags, and accurate video descriptions. Viral videos are eminently compelling and are organically shared to others by viewers. Influencers can even leave their contact information in their viral video's description so that sponsors, media companies, fans, and other influencers can reach out to them.

Ample key factors cause a video to go viral. It goes beyond simply strategically leveraging the utmost ascetically appealing thumbnail and utmost catchy title that resonates with the viewer and entices them to watch the video. It also goes beyond utilizing the utmost optimal and germane long tail keywords and/or short tail keywords for search engine purposes that are applicable to the video's contents. Influencers need to have marketing shrewdness and know how to disseminate their video content onto as many social media platforms as possible for marketing purposes such as, FaceBook, Twitter, Tumblr, and Pineterest, in order to help their videos organically build traction.

They also need their prospective viral video to have a so called wow factor that renders it so enthralling that viewers feel inclined to organically share it with friends and family. It also needs to unique in nature so that it is not easily reproducible by other content creator.

Moreover, the viral video should also be bizarre and organically encourage user activity on the video and an ongoing dialogue in the comments section. For instance, people love watching videos appertaining to supernatural phenomenons since it is a topic people find intriguing, love to discuss and read comments about, and feel inclined to share the excitement about with friends and family members.

Another factor that has bearing on determining whether or not a video goes viral include its level of humorous. The more humour potency a video has, the more apt it is to go viral overtime. For instance, people love watching prank videos and sharing them with their friends and family member. Prank videos are not only cringe worth and bizarre, but they are also extremely humorous and provide ample laughs to the viewers.

Influencers should avail themselves of more collaboration opportunities with other growing influencers so that they can further grow their audience. By creating viral video content, you are more apt to earn more product placement revenue, receive interview requests from media outlets, and even establish a massive loyal following. The benefits of creating viral video content are multitudinous for growing a brand and attaining prominence as an influencer. The implications of creating viral video content are eminently beneficial and bear no adverse effects.

It is salient to create viral video content to grow your brand. By creating video content that has the potential to go viral, you will bolster your brand growth and subscriber growth. You will also be able to reap more monthly donations via Patreon as the increased viewership levels culminates in you earning more patron pledges from new viewers. Moreover, by creating viral video content, you will be more apt to reap more sponsorship revenue and affiliate marketing revenue. Companies love to work with influencers that have attained extreme fame leverage and massive followings of subscribers, especially if influencer's subscriber base is subsumed under the company's target market. Viral videos often have lasting power and provide a means for influencer's to attain substantially increased brand exposure overtime.

As per the fifth step, you will need to profusely, strategically, and enticingly market your brand content to further accelerate your brand growth and gain more traction as an influencer developing a behemoth of a brand. As mentioned prior, similarly to the video game developer, the growing influencer can profusely leveraging social media platforms for content marketing purposes and can even launch affordable pay-per-click campaigns on low cost advertising platforms, such as FaceBook and Instagram, to not only refocus their marketing efforts, but to also attain more targeted reach in a far more cost-effective manner than utilizing traditional marketing strategies. The rising influencer can buy endorsements from world renowned influencers his target market follows for the prospect of more rapidly growing his following by being able to reach out to a greater audience.

As previously mentioned, similarly to the video game developer, the rising influencer can revitalize his marketing efforts to not only draw forth more viewership levels, but to also ensure that he is stretching out his digital marketing dollars as much as possible. The influencer should ensure that his pay-per-click marketing campaigns are targeting the appropriate demographic cohort of viewers subsumed under his brand's target market.

As previously punctuated, the analytical data derived from their marketing campaigns should be meticulously analyzed so that he cannot only refine the marketing campaigns as necessary by removing unprofitable elements, but so that they can also better understand what types of advertisements culminate in eliciting the most conversions. He can work toward optimizing his digital marketing campaigns so that he is able to convert the maximizing the amount of viewers into subscribers per dollar spent.

As mentioned prior, while creating enticing pay-per-click digital market campaigns is beneficial to boost brand growth, the influencer should prioritize organically marketing his brand content so that he does not succumb to a negative return on investment. While it may be beneficial to accelerate brand growth, there is no guarantee that an investment in launching enticing pay-per-click digital market campaigns or buy endorsements from world renowned influencers will culminate in a future positive return on investment even if it allows your brand to gain thousands of new subscribers. The utmost risk adverse influencer without a marketing budget should also primarily take advantage of profusely marketing their brands "on social media platforms, such as Facebook, Twitter, Instagram, Tumblr, and YouTube, at low to no cost" (Totka, 2017) which can help draw forth more brand awareness in a hyper competitive global marketplace.

As previously emphasized, while becoming a highly successful influencer online on social media platforms in the digital era is no easy feat, it is an achievable goal that is viably possible. Accomplishing this meritorious feat of becoming a highly successful influencer online on social media platforms is possible for those who are able to consistency create compelling, share worthy content subsumed under their niche content genre and is also possible for those who are able to demonstrate unalloyed determination, unremitting strategic hard work, and profound marketing effectiveness. Becoming a highly successful influencer online on social media platforms is a cumbersome undertaking that can take 10,000s of hours or ample years of indefatigable strategic hard work for even the utmost dedicated and determined individuals.

The plethora of disparate benefits appertaining to becoming a successful influencer online and attaining extreme fame leverage can profoundly augment every facet of your life, especially when earning money is no longer a cumbersome process, but rather a seamless process. By being able to obtain the wealth overtime as a renowned influencer, you are able to liberate your time and focus in on what truly matters in life instead of being fettered by working spirit crushing, time draining, disheartening, dead end, minimum wage that do not even offer any semblance of a sustenance wage.

As mentioned prior, individuals that have attained extreme fame leverage, even those whom are not reputed as leading industry experts, are able to generate more revenue in a single hour than the average person will earn working throughout the entirety of their life. For instance, "at the 2018 10X Growth Conference hosted by Grant Cardone and Russell Brunson, the co-founder of Clickfunnels, were able to sell $3,2000,000 in 90 minutes on stage" (Nanor, 2018). Influencers with massive followings without even any hard skills can also generate more revenue in a couple minutes by producing a single Instagram than the average person will earn working throughout the entirety of their lifetime. For instance, "Kylie Jenner commands $1,000,000 per Instagram post, with Gomez in second at $800,000 per post" (Vanderberg, 2018). The importance of building a robust brand to establish yourself as a content creator and influencer so that you can draw forth a lucrative following on social media platforms is often overlooked over working a traditional, dead end job with no high paying career prospects.

It was reported that "Ryan, a-then-7 year old content creator, made $11 million from his YouTube channel, coming in at number 8 on Forbes' 2017 list. His YouTube channel has attracted a huge following of parents and children who watch Ryan test out new toys and share his thoughts on them" (O'Kane, 2018). He is in fact so successful at creating a lucrative brand around his passion that he has earned more revenue in one month at the tender age of 7 than the average STEM degree holder will ever earn working multiple jobs throughout the entirely of their lifetime. When individuals begin to work from a young age on developing brands around their passions and interests, the outcomes can render them poised for unprecedented success as adults, especially if they already have amassed ample entrepreneurial work experience and already built lucrative brands during their childhood years which they can further grow amid their adulthood years. The benefits of becoming an influencer amid your childhood translate into you being able to attain unprecedented wealth as a young adult. Ryan even has an entire toy line named after his whimsical life, called Ryan's World, that can be found in major retail stores, such as Target and Walmart.

As previously punctuated, attention is undoubtedly the new currency of the digital era. Millennials emphatically understand the importance of entrepreneurship and brand building to attain wealth from selling product placements, earning royalties, and generating advisement revenue. Moreover, millennial content creators and influencers also understand the importance of brand build so that they eventually receive subscription revenue, generate sponsorship revenue, and reap monthly Patreon donations from patrons. Individuals who are successful in the real world as children in the social media landscape are preordained to attain profound financial success as adults.

By becoming a successful influencer online and attaining extreme fame leverage, you will be able to liberate your time, never have to struggle to earn money, and focus on reaching your higher aspirations, optimizing your health, and helping others. The benefits that becoming a successful influencer online and attaining extreme fame leverage confers to the renowned influencer are endless since there are unlimited possibilities to how you can advance your life when you have full purview over your time and have the wealth to render your dreams into reality.

The plethora of assorted benefits of becoming a successful influencer online and attaining extreme fame leverage on social media platforms are profound. First and foremost, by becoming an influencer, you will be able to substantially increase your revenue and earning potential. Influencers are not relegated to their earnings potential being limited by a pittance of a fixed amount of fiat currency from a dead-end, minimum wage job that does not even offer a sustenance wage for affording housing. Influencers can draw forth affiliate marketing revenue, sponsorship marketing revenue, subscription revenue, royalties, advertisement revenue, and donations. Influencers earn revenue every time a donation is received via Muxy, Streamlabs, Twitch cheers, or Patreon.

For example, live streamer and influencer Ice Poseidon was able to earn over $5000 purely in an 8 hour period through donations by live streaming himself sleeping. Amid this live stream, viewers would keep submitting $100+ donations in an attempt to wake him up by having media sharing donations and text to speech donations play from Streamlabs. Donations are the currency to mold the streamer's future content, interact with the streamer, or elicit their thoughts about a particular topic.

Additionally, influencers generate affiliate marketing revenue by referring their viewers to purchasable products and receive a commission on every referred sale which can be purely profitable on the influencer's end. Content creators and influencers for instance can join affiliate programs and recommend for their viewers to buy products via their Amazon affiliate links (Stephenson, 2019) or eBay affiliate links to draw forth additional passive income streams.

Influencers can earn an exorbitant amount of subscription revenue on YouTube and Twitch from their paid subscribers and can also draw forth a copious amount of advertisement revenue from their viewers who watch their monetized content. Furthermore, influencers can charge exorbitant product placement fees, sometimes in the hundreds of thousands of dollars, just to simply feature a company's product in their video. Influencers can also earn millions of dollars in sponsorship revenue by endorsing a brand. Rodger Federer for instance received over $86,000,000 in endorsement revenue (Badenhausen, 2019) in 2019 alone. "In addition to his blockbuster Uniqlo pact, Federer added a multimillion-dollar deal with Rimowa last year. The luggage brand joined Credit Suisse, Mercedes-Benz, Rolex, Moet & Chandon, Barilla and others in Federer's endorsement stable" (Badenhausen, 2019).

Second, by becoming an influencer you will be able to receive an exorbitant amount of products and access to ample subscription based services for free. Brands are keen on sponsoring influencers so that influencers can spread awareness of the brand's product offerings and service offerings. Influencers are able to save money by availing themselves of access to products and subscription based services that they would otherwise have to pay off if they did not have enormous followings on social media platforms. "Brands are becoming more and more interested in an Influencer's overall goals, the authenticity of their following, and the value of the content being published" (*"5 Benefits Of,"* 2018). An investment in influencer marketing can yield a higher return on investment than more traditional forms of marketing, especially if the influencer's following is part of the brand's target market. Customers are far more apt to buy products recommended by influencers who they follow, trust, and have formed a virtual connection with by having vicariously experienced their life through frequently watching the influencer's social media content.

Third, another profound benefit appertaining to becoming an influencer is that you will have the chance to transform peoples' live, inspire others, help communities, and make a difference in the world in a positive manner. "People look to influencers for inspiration, advice, or to help guide their sense of fashion. The list goes on. It is incredibly important to be aware of this, and have a solid understanding of the things you could say or do that may cause the loyalty of your followers to diminish" (*"5 Benefits Of,"* 2018).

In other to attain profound success as an upcoming influencer you will need to earn it based on your own merits and the worthiness of your brand content. Once you have attained success as an influencer on your own, you will be able to reach a greater audience when you disseminate knowledge to others, bequeath new skills to others, and help others resolve persisting issues. Additionally, you will be able to make positive changes in the world as a renowned followers since your meritorious goals will be heard by millions and your followers will also be financially supportive of the worthwhile causes you support.

Influencers for instance have the clout needed to raise millions of dollars for charities and can play a major role in helping to make a difference in struggling peoples' lives by financially helping them to overcome hardships and struggles. People looks to influencers for inspiration and are inclined to pay it forward when they witness their favorite influencers helping to enrich communities and the lives of individuals in some capacity, such as donating to charities that feed the homeless.

Fourth, becoming an influencer provides profound opportunities for learning, growth, and development. As an influencer, you will organically assimilate pragmatic knowledge and first-hand experience appertaining to how to be successful in the current economic climate. This is because, you will need to provide lofty economic value to your target market in order to be successful as an influencer. Evolving your brand to the next level will require you to learn the utmost optimal influencer marketing practices and will also mandate you to tap into your mental bandwidth and exhaust your creative potential in order to be able to churn out more enticing and compelling, novel content that provides unprecedented value to your target market.

Becoming an influencer can elicit a fulfilling, hectic, and opportune life. As a successful influencer, you will have the ability to meet other influencers, attain lucrative endorsement deals from brands, and explore ample opportunities for brand growth. As you build more traction as a successful influencer, you will cultivate a larger following, development more skill sets, amass more pragmatic knowledge, build more revenue streams, and secure more endorsement deals.

By becoming an influencer, you can monetize your passions and hobbies, and turn something that was once costly into a full time, highly profitable, fulfilling career that you created on your own out of nothing. Becoming an influencer can profoundly change your life in every facet, especially as you become more of a world renowned expert of your niche field, profusely grow your following, inspire more people, and actualize your high aspirations into a reality.

As an renowned influencer who has attained extreme fame leverage, "you will have a platform to learn, expand, and introduce new subject matter into your content. The more variety of useful content you can provide to your followers, the more you can grow your social media influencer network" ("*5 Benefits of*," 2018). By becoming a successful influencer online and attaining extreme fame leverage, not only can you enhance every aspect of your life, but you can also leverage your clout in order to help others thrive, prosper, and flourish. The plethora of assorted benefits of becoming a successful influencer online and attaining extreme fame leverage preponderantly outweigh living a life as an employee in all facets.

Earning substantial money online to be able to afford to eminently enrich every aspect of your life, take control of your work life, and even become an influencer is also more viable than ever before. This is because, it is easier today than anytime in history for influencers to generate revenue online and take control of their lives as they are in the early stages of building their brands, even if they do not have the luxury of creating brand content full time before their brands begin to build substantial traction. In other words, the prospective influencer never has to concede to working a dispiriting, time draining, dead end, minimum wage job that does not even pay a sustenance wage for affording housing. The rising influencer has the option to leverage his high income skills to provide his with substantial revenue when his brand is nascent in its initial months and not bringing in any revenue. The rising influencer is often a full time content creator in some capacity, but also has high income skills that he can also leverage to generate substantial revenue as he is in the initial phases of growing his brand.

In the digital era, it is more viable than anytime in history to attain high income skills even if you lack the requisite financial resources to afford a college education. It is incumbent to attain high income skills if you plan on providing substantial marketplace value to clients by creating a lucrative niche brand. Attaining high income skills can also be salient if you plan on building a professional reputation and sizeable clientele so that you can command a lofty salary. Some of the ample high income skills that do not mandate any degrees nor certifications encompass high ticket closing, copywriting, paid speaking, consulting, coaching, programming, and digital marketing skills.

Attaining these high income skills goes beyond simply watching hundreds of tutorial videos on YouTube and reading insightful eBooks appertaining to mastering these high income skills. It also involves capitalizing on opportunities to practice these high income skills, listening to audio books appertaining to how to enhance these skills, and finding mentors that can bequeath these skills to you in addition to offering you guidance beyond what can be gleaned from educational books or videos. Experiential learning is perhaps the utmost efficacious way for someone to proficiently master a high income skill since theoretical learning is far less conducive to cultivating long term memories than pragmatically applying knowledge through first-hand experiences.

Someone interested in mastering the trade of copywriting for instance can watch copywriting video tutorials on YouTube, read educational eBooks appertaining to copywriting via Kindle Unlimited, can access copywriting audio books through through the Audible application on their smart phone while traveling, and can also attain a mentorship in order to ascertain how to bolster his copywriting skills to the next level. Having a mentor to serve as a role analyst figure does more than just simply helps motivate and guide the mentee throughout his arduous journey in the workforce. The mentor also can directly address any inquiries his mentee might have that have been unresolved.

Being a practitioner is perhaps the utmost efficacious way to learn something since first-hand experience is far more conducive to developing long-term memories than theoretical learning which unfortunately more often than not does not culminate in forming long-term memories. This is because, your mind has no need to develop long-term memories and retain non-pragmatic knowledge in the form of theoretical knowledge which is far less recallable, especially if it cannot be experienced. The practitioner mastering copywriting should be executing email marketing strategies, refining product descriptions to render them more enticing, and should be curating more social media marketing content to elicit more product sales. Copywriting involves enticing the target market to buy products and unequivocally extends simply beyond creating shrewd social media posts to promote a product in the digital era.

Copywriters can work as freelancers remotely and build their own clientele. They need to understand how to most efficaciously enhance their verbiage so that it more profoundly resonates with their target market and more succinctly communicates that the advertised products can remedy outstanding problems. Even though customers dread being sold to, they ineffably love buying products. The market will determine the merits of the copywriter's advertisement content based on the sales results. Through amassing an exorbitant amount of first-hand experiences copywriting, the copywriter will refine his skills overtime by learning how to more enticingly indirectly sell to customers through persuasive copywriting. All major brands need to curate content on social media platforms in order to generate product awareness and win over the customer's trust and patronage. Profusely executing digital marketing activities is paramount so that brands can maintain a constant presence in the customer's mind.

Brands cannot remain profitable if they can easily be forgotten about or are overshadowed by other competitor brands who more aggressively market their similar products. Copywriters are needed so that brands can render the utmost profitable sales results out of quality advertisements which deliver unprecedented value by communicating a simple solution to unresolved problems, while also being easily understandable, memorable, and eminently consistent with the company's brand image. Experiential learning is perhaps the utmost effective way for a copywriter to master his rhetoric, hone his copywriting skills, and become a top tier copywriter as he enriches his understanding of the utmost efficacious copywriting practices to exhibit overtime simply by applying them. Copywriting is one of the utmost pragmatic, high income skills to master that you help you generate a six figure income and work in virtually any industry of your choice that leverages digital marketing activities and needs more copywriters.

Another high income skills someone can master without any semblance of a post-secondary education entails high ticket closing which involves reaping a commission of one thousand dollars or more every time you sell a product as a high ticket closer. Honing your persuasion skills, communication skills, social skills, sales skills, and business acumen will play a pivotal role in helping you become a stellar high ticket closer. People buy from professionals they trust, respect, and befriended. Closing a sale for a high ticket item in which you reap an exorbitant commission from can involve selling real estate, yachts, and even vehicles. High ticket closers can watch educational closing videos online, read informative closing eBooks and insightful articles in order to ascertain pragmatic knowledge about the utmost potent closing techniques. High ticket closers are often able to perform their job remotely to close sales.

A third high income skill involves engaging in paid speaking opportunities as you are becoming a renowned expert in your niche field. "Paid speakers can also double as platform closers. Platforms closers are speakers who sell products or services on stages to an audience. Getting hundreds or thousands of people to buy a product can be a daunting, nerve racking task when you do not know how to do it" (Nanor, 2018). Honing public speaking skills involves enrolling in free public speaking courses and joining public speaking groups on Meetup to learn how to overcome public speaking anxiety and master your public speaking skills. Moreover, paid public speakers can also learn about the best public speaking techniques by listening to insightful public speaking podcasts, watching educational public speaking videos, and by reading insightful articles and eBooks appertaining to the best public speaking practices to leverage. Additionally, prospective paid public speakers can even garner constructive criticism from audience members to identify areas for improvement. The advent of webinars and live streaming has allowed paid public speakers to work remotely online.

    A fourth high income skill entails working as a consultant or coach. Consultants and coaches are highly valued for being able to elicit profound results for their clients. Consultants are solution providers and are able to parlay their knowledge they accrued as experts in their respective niche fields into delivering meaningful and pragmatic solutions to their clients. Being able to become a high paid consultant involves creating a personalized brand to market yourself as an industry expert, curating content on social media platforms appertaining to your niche area of expertise, and building a robust professional network.

As a consultant, you can set your hourly rates, work remotely, develop your own professional website, and keep updated with the utmost efficacious industry practices to leverage through watching insightful videos, reading informative articles and eBooks, and listening to educational podcasts to amplify your knowledge base. You can also glean insights about changes to your field and what industry practices should be executed by conversing with other industry experts at networking events. Moreover, you are also apt to receive more client referrals from other professionals overtime as you build up a robust professional network and become reputed as leading and illustrious expert in your niche field on social media platforms. Some consultants are even able to generate a seven figure salary since they know how to resolve outstanding business issues and streamline business models to render them far more profitable.

A more recent desirable high income skill set involves attaining digital marketing skills. Understanding how to implement the utmost efficacious practices in the areas of content marketing, email marketing, pay per click marketing campaigns, social media marketing, search engine optimize (SEO), and context marketing will allow you to have valuable, high income skill sets that brands need to stay ahead of their competition. The digital marketing landscape is exponentially growing as more and more marketing dollars are earmarked into digital marketing efforts over traditional marketing efforts.

"Digital marketing agencies are a very popular way to start making $10,000 a month because you can charge business owners and individuals $1,0000—$10,000 a month just to mange their online advertising and help them rank higher on Google's search engine algorithm. You can also help them grow their brand and following so that they can generate them more sales online" (Nanor, 2018). Attaining digital marketing skills involves more than just being a practitioner and finding a mentor figure. It also involves enrolling in free digital marketing courses, listening to educational digital marketing podcasts, watching insightful digital marketing videos, and reading informative articles and eBooks appertaining to the utmost effective digital marketing to leverage. Digital marketers also have the luxury of being able to work remotely.

A sixth high income skill set that is perhaps the utmost cumbersome to master includes attaining programming skill. It is unnecessary to enroll in a coding boot camp to learn coding languages nor markup languages. Prospective coders can take free coding courses, listen to educational coding podcasts, watch insightful coding tutorial videos, and read informative articles and eBooks appertaining to programming. By learning ample programming languages, such as Python and Javascript, coders will have highly valuable skills and will be able to develop digital products, websites, games, and even applications for companies. Coding is a hard skill that is highly in demand and can warrant the pursuit of mastering since the skill can be extremely profitable to posses as part of your skill repertoire. Coders can watch thousands of hours of YouTube coding tutorial videos and can learn the utmost in-demand program languages. prospective singers should also master the markup languages, such as HTML, XML, and XHTML, and should practice coding problems to further enhance their coding skills.

The importance of mastering high income skills should not be overlooked. This is because, high income skills are not only in-demand by employers, but can also allow you to thrive as a freelancer or build a lucrative brand around these high income skills. Moreover, high income skills are versatile skill sets which can translate to allowing you to pivot to working in another field if you want a career change. For instance, a singer working on web development for a retailer's website can pivot to working on video game development or manufactured application development for another company, presuming they possess the requisite coding skills to complete the entrepreneurial pursuits. Coders can often completely their job functions remotely.

Earning a six figure income through mastering high income skills is easier in the digital era than anytime in history, especially if you leverage the global digital distribution power of social media platforms to build a lucrative personalized brand and establish yourself as an industry expert. For instance, an adept, autodidact coder can parlay his knowledge into creating educational coding tutorial videos on YouTube and can also produce insight programming podcasts. Moreover, he can write informative articles and eBooks appertaining to how to master coding. Furthermore, he can also create automated online courses and develop the modules in order to teach others the basics and intricacies of coding. He can utilize these income generating assets he created to draw forth multiple sources of revenue, such as advertisement revenue and sponsorship revenue from videos, subscription revenue from paid subscribers, tuition revenue from online course sales, and royalties from selling eBooks. The coder can also offer consultancy services and set his hourly rate to at least $1000 an hour if he has attained extreme fame leverage as a leading industry expert across multiple social media platforms.

Earning a six figure income by leveraging high income, in-demand skills becomes far more viable as you grow a robust personalized brand that provides unprecedented value to prospective clients and that is able to efficaciously market yourself as a leading industry expert. In other words, beyond working for clients and companies on an hourly basis or per project basis, you should not only focus on growing your personalized brand by substantially increasing your valuable content reservoir, but should also build a professional network so that you can one day reap a seven figure income from having far more leverage and clout as prolific industry expert in your niche field. Leverage high income skills to make substantial money online is more viable in the digital era than ever before, especially if you become renowned as an industry expert in your niche field.

As mentioned prior, individuals with extreme fame leverage, even those that are not reputed as leading industry experts, are able to generate more revenue in a single hour than the average person will earn working throughout the entirety of their life. For instance, "at the 2018 10X Growth Conference hosted by Grant Cardone and Russell Brunson, the co-founder of Clickfunnels, were able to sell $3,2000,000 in 90 minutes on stage" (Nanor, 2018). Influencers with massive followings without even any hard skills can also generate more revenue in a couple minutes by producing a single Instagram than the average person will earn working throughout the entirety of their lifetime. For instance, as previously punctuated, "Kylie Jenner commands $1,000,000 per Instagram post, with Gomez in second at $800,000 per post" (Vanderberg, 2018). The importance of building a personalized brand to establish yourself as a leading industry expert and draw forth a lucrative following on social media platforms is often overlooked over working a traditional job with no high paying career prospects.

The ability to generate multiple streams of income by mastering these high income skills and subsequently creating ample educational, monetizable content appertaining to theses income skills is often overlooked. Out of all the aforementioned high income skills that do not require degrees, coding is perhaps the utmost lucrative skill to master. For instance, "Mark Zuckerberg became a billionaire by developing apps and Evan Spiegel is the second youngest billionaire, after Kylie Jenner because he created a social media app" (Nanor, 2018). With the ability to create a brand oriented around these high income skills, the earnings potential are uncapped and are potentially limitless since you are not confined to relinquishing your finite time for a fixed amount of money based on an hourly in the digital era.

Creating a niche brand that can potentially reach out to over 8 billion people with the global digital distribution power of social media platforms can be far more lucrative overtime than you envisioned, especially if you also attain extreme fame leverage as a leading industry expert. Selling a single product placement may render you more income in a single day than you may have otherwise earned throughout the totality of the previous decades, assuming your brand has millions of followers apart of the advertiser's target market. Having extreme fame leverage even allows speakers to command over $200,000 for delivering a single speech, such as Tony Robbins and Mark Cuban. Donald Trump for instance commands at least $1,500,000 dollars per speech (Nanor, 2018) as a speaking fee. Those who have attained utmost extreme leverage have the highest earnings potential since they have instant access and clout over a massive loyal following that brands need to be able to reach through advertisements, product placements, and sponsors.

As previously punctuated, since the job prospects as a future employee are so grim and bleak for college graduates, it seems as though the only viable career prospect in a hyper competitive marketplace is being a full-time entrepreneur. Allocating thousands of hours applying for low paying jobs is an unwarranted, loss of time investment. This is because, the search for a job simply bears an enormous opportunity cost. The precious time squandered on completing meaningless job applications can be otherwise earmarked towards fostering a potentially profitable brand with no earnings cap.

As previously mentioned, college students and graduate students have unresolved qualms about their major educational decisions. It is disconcerting to hear that auto mechanics succumb to being pizza delivery drivers, doctors succumb to working as day labors on farms, and lawyers even concede to being Uber drivers in order to generate income in the digital era. If earning a college degree, graduate degree, or even a doctorate cannot even help you attain a job, then it is unequivocally worthless in the real world.

As mentioned prior, graduates come to realization that their academic efforts were eminently fruitless and that they squandered at least one fourth of their life without being able to reap anything in return for their efforts. These qualms will be all the more agonizing and devastating when they come to the realization that they could have otherwise been growing a lucrative brand online and creating ample income generating assets to profusely expand their brand's content reservoir so that they could be far closer towards having a prosperous future from a young age. Unlike something as inexpensive as a small toy that has resale value on the second hand market, a piece of paper in the form of a degree is unequivocally worthless and offers absolutely no resale value to graduates.

Expanding your network in the digital era will present you with far more opportunities to meet more people which can result in seamlessly finding more prospective future partners as you grow your personalized brand, clout, and network. In other words, prospective future partners will be less challenging to find as you become more successful and attain more leverage overtime from growing your personalized brand, influence, and professional network. People in general have a proclivity to be highly attracted to successful, highly influential individuals since they are perceived as offering tremendous value to others. The outcome of being highly successful may even culminate in prospective future partners you encounter being the utmost adoring fans of your personalized brand content.

Building a robust network in the digital era is easier than ever before by leveraging the global distribution power of social media networks and organized events through Meetup. Meetup is a service which not only hosts a plethora of in-person events, but also offers a myriad of online groups that individuals can join. People that join online Meetup groups and attend in-person Meetup events typically have an interest in the hobbies that the Meetup groups are oriented around. Meetup groups are free to join and Meetup events are typically almost always free to attend.

Meetup events can be found locally and provide non-intrusive opportunities for professionals to build a robust network. By joining a Meetup group and subsequently attending their events, you will not only be in a friendly environment with a relaxed ambiance where you can expand your knowledge base through learning from others, but also will be able to capitalize on the opportunity to connect with an exorbitant amount of people. During these Meetup group events, it is easy to establish yourself as a trustworthy and reputable individual by connecting with other attendees through meaningful discussions appertaining to the area of common interest the Meetup group revolves around.

Once you have attained the trust of other attendees through meaningful conversions, you can begin to position yourself as a subject matter expert in your niche area of expertise. "Of course, all of that goes along with you boosting your professional reputation. One really important thing that you need to understand is that boosting your reputation will not happen overnight. It will take time, patience, and effort" (Cohn, n.d.).

During the Meetup sessions, it is important to establish trustworthiness and build credibility as a professional. It is important to naturally build your professional reputation overtime and not solicit others to provide you with business. This way, you can come across as professional, reputable, and trustworthy rather than being perceived as a solicitor. You do not want to gain notoriety for being perceived as sleazy, sordid, disreputable, or unprofessional. By abstaining from soliciting business from others at Meetup events and instead focusing on forming lasting connections by providing meaningful insights through conversations with other professionals, it is inevitable that overtime you will eventually be inquired about your credentials. When asked about your background, you can then subsequently capitalize on the opportune moment to "position yourself as the subject matter expert in your area of expertise. At Meetup events you have the potential to encounter all sorts of interesting people with whom you may one day do business" (Cohn, n.d.).

You can also have business cards at your disposal and provide them when asked at Meetup events. Moreover, you can even go one step further by providing others with a copy of your book to help solidify your perceived merits as an industry expert. Books can be a powerful tool for distinguishing yourself from other professionals and books will render your personalized brand far more memorable since books occupy a spot on the prospective client's shelf and are unlikely to be disposed of, unlike business cards. Prospective clients that are provided with a free book from you will be far more apt to procure consultation services from you if they need a consultant since you have already proven your expertise to them and have organically established meaningful connections with them through Meetup events. An investment in dispensing free books at Meetup events can bare a substantial return on investment since books not only have lasting power and prove your expertise in a niche area, but also are able to help you gain more clients. The marketing investment of doling out free books at events can be warranted, especially if it can have significant bearing on bringing in more clients and even referrals from those who received the books. Unlike paid advertisements, books do not simply perish after being viewed or after an advertisement budget for a pay-per-click marketing campaign has been depleted.

By organically creating meaningful connections through attending Meetup events, you not only build a robust professional network overtime, but may also gain referrals from other professionals that you established lasting connections with from having consistently attended Meetup events. When you are perceived as a credible, reputable, trustworthy, and approachable expert in your niche, you are more likely to gain referrals from others who you were able to provide valuable insights to at the events, such as the utmost effective and latest industry practices that businesses should utilize. Attending Meetup events to engage with people who share similar interests to you can be a worthwhile long term investment for organically building a robust professional network overtime. Meetup groups can range from something as celestial as astronomy to something as pragmatic as entrepreneurship being the key focus of the Meetup group events.

The benefits of attending Meetup events are multitudinous and extend beyond the opportunity to build a robust professional network. By attending Meetup events, you can ascertain more insights appertaining to your niche field of interest from knowledge individuals. Moreover, by attending Meetup events, you can improve your social skills and public speaking skills, attain more meaningful life experiences, foster more long term friendships, further cultivate your personalized brand by establishing yourself as a trustworthy professional, and possibly even elicit new career opportunities. "The more you give to the Meetup group, the more you will get out of it, in terms of the relationships and opportunities. Shell for instance found a job when one of the members of his group learned he had been laid off. The group member was so impressed with his presentations. If you add value to the Meetup members consistently over time then it will likely pay dividends" (Spencer, 2014).

Starting a Meetup group is highly beneficial for personalized brand building and also presents an outlet for public speaking opportunities in which you can establish yourself as a knowledge industry expert. Starting a Meetup group on a computer through Meetup.com simply involves "selecting start a new group in the top navigation bar and following the steps to customize your new Meetup group. You can then select an organizer subscription plan. Meetup groups are community focused, local, and create ongoing opportunities for members to" (*"How do I,"* n.d.) interact with one another in-person and learn from each other.

Starting your own Meetup group from Meetup's manufactured website on your smart phone entails "tapping the groups icon in the top navigation bar and then selecting start a Meetup group. Once you have completed the aforementioned tasks, you can then select get started and subsequently proceed to following the requisite steps in order to customize your new Meetup group before selecting an organizer subscription plan" (*"How do I,"* n.d.).

To render your Meetup groups more compelling, you can invite guest speakers and provide refreshments. You can host the Meetup groups at the library or some other public venue. "You can also choose to structure the meeting so that you have open networking at the beginning, feature a presenter, and also have another networking opportunity after the presentation is finished. That is a common approach for many networking meetings, which seems to work well" (Cohn, n.d.). Once you have established your reputation as an industry expert, you can refer the attendees to enroll in your courses and read your eBooks online to learn more about the presented topics of interest. Hosting Meetup events not only helps your personalized brand build traction and allows you to expand your professional network, but also can lead to more public speaking opportunities on other platforms, such as radio shows and podcasts, as more people reach out to you with interview requests. Moreover, you can customize how you want to structure your Meetup event so that it does not have to be like a typical unfruitful networking event. Your Meetup events can encourage ample audience participation and meaningful group interactions.

The inherent value that traditional networking events offer jobseekers has become egregiously overly embellished. Attending traditional networking events will not only have absolutely no bearing on you attaining a desirable job, but will also adversely impinge on your self-esteem and self-confidence as you are hurled right back to square one after being disillusioned by the outcome of attending the overpriced networking event. There are ample reason as to why you should not squander your sacrosanct time attending network events beyond the aforementioned reasons provided.

First, it is almost impossible to find a prospective employer at a networking event since the bulk of attendees are jobseekers and not employers. "Another drawback is that many attendees treat these networking sessions primarily as a pickup place" (Sullivan, 2018). Moreover, another issue simply lies in needing to converse with a copious amount of people at a networking event before you are fortunate enough to stumble upon one of the few that might possibly be able to help you attain a job. In other words, attending a networking event can be a veritably inefficacious approach to attaining a job.

Second, it can be eminently arduous to identify who you should be interacting with since there is no easy way for attendees to distinguish employers apart from jobseekers without first interacting with as many people as possible. Unlike a career fair, prospective employers at these networking events will not have booths and be easily identifiable among the throng. "Many jobseekers inadvertently spend most of their time drinking, eating, or talking to other jobseekers or disinterested professionals" (Sullivan, 2018).

Third, employers attending networking events may advertently avoid jobseekers in favor of conversing with employed professionals. Professionals attending networking events would often prefer to confer with other professionals so that they can learn the latest and utmost efficacious industry practices. They will likely find it vexing when jobseekers solicit them for job opportunities and career advice. "Moreover, jobseekers frequently bring nothing more than a paper resume and a business card. Jobseekers do not go to the event completely up-to-date in their field and ready to share best practices" (Sullivan, 2018). This culminates in jobseekers not offering any real value to established professionals interested in ascertaining the latest result driven strategies and tactics for success in their niche field.

Fourth, another overlooked issue with networking events is that in-depth conversations are unlikely to transpire since "the room is almost always noisy and there is seldom any place to sit and hold an in-depth, extended conversation" (Sullivan, 2018). Furthermore, during networking events in which a speaker provides a presentation, there is little to no time to converse nor mingle. These impediments not only renders the event unavailing for aspiring employees, but also still leaves them jobless and without any new contacts after the event has elapsed.

Fifth, these networking events can behighly time consuming consuming as well as exorbitantly expensive to attend. Event admission fees can be costly and add up quickly, ultimately causing the jobseeker to succumb to a steep negative return on investment from attending these events. Additionally, the networking session may also not be within a close vicinity to the jobseeker's address which unfortunately defeats the overarching purpose of attending the events if the best outcome is that the jobsite for a prospective work opportunity is in a distant city that the jobseeker is unwilling to commute to each workday.

Sixth, jobseekers attending these networking events typically go there in a desultory manner without specific career goals nor a hyper-focused job search pitch planned. This lack of planning can adversely impact their reputation, "especially if they appear desperate by obviously handing out business cards or resumes indiscriminately to everyone. Many also fail to ask questions after the formal presentation, therefore missing an opportunity to be highly visible. And many others fail to follow up after the event, completely losing any of the initial value that may have been gained" (Sullivan, 2018). Jobseekers at these network events are also unable to deliver a hyper-focused job search pitch to prospective employers that elucidates how they can provide long term value to their company and eminently fulfill their needs. Instead, their job search pitch is unable to garner interest since it is too self-centered rather than being strategically employer oriented. Jobseekers are typically ill-prepared to properly present themselves to prospective employers and need to meticulously understanding the employer's needs and perspective to market themselves more effectively.

If you attend a traditional networking event without proper preparation, it will culminate in being a fruitless endeavour since someone is not going to dedicate anytime to helping you with your job search (Sullivan, 2018) predicament if you cannot demonstrate any significant long term value you can offer employers over other prospective employees. Employers do not want to settle for less and are looking to hire individuals who are the most experienced, competent, skilled, and who can articulate their merits eminently well.

Similarly to attending traditional networking events, attending career fairs may also culminate in being a sheer and waste of time for the average attendee. Career fairs attract massive competition and recent college graduates which ultimately positions the unemployed at a greater disadvantage than at networking events. Moreover, due to the congestion of unemployed attendees, there is no time to develop, meaningful conversations with recruiters. Recruiters will even often times refer jobseekers to the company website to fill out the job application. The recruiters attending the career fairs that accept resumes in person are almost always the gatekeepers to landing an actual job interview. Unfortunately, "the best thing they can do is put your resume in a 'good' pile. It is the first step in a long funnel of hiring" (Sullivan, 2018) since they are not the hiring managers.

The positions career fair jobs recruiters are looking for prospective job candidates to fulfill are often low paying, entry level jobs. Since firms dispatch rookie recruiters, it is unlikely that you would be able to learn more about the low paying position by speaking to a career fair recruiter than you could otherwise find by browsing the company's website. "If you are unemployed and your experience and training are dated, you might find that even rookie recruiters simply will not want to talk to you because their hiring managers may be prejudiced against the unemployed" (Sullivan, 2018). Career fairs are typically unattended by hiring managers and prospective employees are often required to apply for positions online which renders these career fairs eminently insignificant towards helping jobseekers attain a position at a company. Furthermore, these minimum wage jobs often do not pay a subsistence wage for a solo income earner. Some of these sales jobs advertised at career fairs are so abysmal that they may pay entirely off of commissions which is typically almost always far worse than receiving an hourly minimum wage since commissions are not guaranteed for your time investment. Attending networking events and career fairs for the average unemployed attendee is preordained to almost always elicit an unfruitful outcome.

Fortunately, there are strategies that can be executed to effectively build a robust professional network. First, establishing a strong professional network entails gaining extreme leverage on social media platforms. This means developing a personalized brand and being an expert in a niche field that others can trust and turn to when referencing meritorious content. Once you have built up the content reservoir comprised of insightful, meaningful content revolving around your area of expertise, you will not only begin gaining a sizeable following, but will also likely be inundated with solicited requests, especially if you parlay your extreme fame leverage into establishing yourself as a consultant. Content creation can include creating insightful videos, writing informative articles, producing educational podcasts and meaningful books.

You will be able to build up your network rapidly when you deliver unprecedented value to the marketplace and utilize social media platforms to globally digital distribute your insightful content. This wealth of meritorious content provided to the marketplace not only helps build your reputation, but also prove your merits as an industry expert. Your network will more rapidly grow as more and more individual contact you to develop mutually beneficial professional relationships rather than you needing to reach out to them.

The second strategy to grow your professional network to the next tier involves engaging in public speaking presentations, establishing online courses, and even offering webinars. When you are providing public speaking presentations, all the attention is honed in onto the speaker. These opportunities to mentor students, hone your public speaking skills, and provide more value to the marketplace beyond an online context, not only further bolsters your reputation as an industry expert, but also provides helps you further organically build your network. As your students attain profound success as professionals and provide you with phenomenal testimonials, it will further render you more appealing to other professionals as an industry expert to follow. Your network will further grow especially as your successful subordinates begin mentoring others and begin referencing your expertise and content to others more frequently. As you build traction as an industry expert and grow your network to the next tier, you will begin to become more selective of who you choose to take on as clients, mentors, and spend time collaborating with. Professionals are attracted to industry experts they can learn from who have a proven track record for attaining profound success in their niche area of expertise. Being able mentor highly successful students and mold them into becoming industry experts speaks volumes about your merits as a leading industry expert.

The third strategy to grow your professional network involves gaining profound publicity. This involves accepting interview requests from media conglomerates, leading industry experts with massive followings, and renowned influencers apart of your niche field. This will ultimately allow your professional network to evolve to the next level by able to potentially garner far more attention than ever before since you will not only have the referrals from other leading industry experts and renowned influencers, but will also attract the attention of a broader audience to your personalized brand content. When you accept interview requests, you cannot only substantially grow your audience, but can also foster a much stronger professional reputation if you are being interviewed by media conglomerates, leading industry experts, and renowned influencers with enormous followings that feel inclined to follow your content.

Building a robust professional network can take ample years since it is eminently time consuming to build up the meritorious content reservoir, gain significant traction, and foster a strong reputation to be perceived as an industry expert from your insightful content, professionals referrals, and ample highly satisfied client testimonials. By creating insightful videos, writing informative articles, publishing meaningful books, churning out educational podcasts, providing valuable online courses, offering pragmatic presentations, having highly successful subordinates, and by accepting interview requests from media conglomerates and other industry experts with massive followings, rapidly building your network will be a much more expeditious process as other professionals reach out to you rather than you needing to contact them.

Building an extraordinary personalized brand to establish yourself as an industry expert in fields, such as business, marketing, and entrepreneurship, in order to establish a sizeable following and strong professional network, can take tens of thousands of hours and years of hard work, self-discipline, unalloyed dedicated, and unwavering determination. However, once you achieved this goal you will no longer be the one soliciting connect requests on LinkedIn, but will rather be the one receiving interview requests, consultation requests, collaboration requests, and connect requests. If your content, products, and services have enough merit, the market will respond accordingly, and you will be deemed an indispensable asset to the marketplace that other people want to conduct business with.

As previously punctuated, having extreme fame leverage as an industry expert with a massive following can be critical for not only building a strong professional network in the digital era, but for also generating significant wealth since attention is the highly sought after currency of the digital era that is constantly being arbitraged by brands. In other words, organically growing a massive following can be an extremely profitable long term time investment, especially once you have attained extreme fame leverage which you can parlay into eliciting multiple lucrative revenue generation opportunities.

Earning substantial revenue as an inexperienced entrepreneur, prospective influencer, prospective investor, or even as a full time college student, graduate student, or doctoral student, without any work experience, is easier today in the digital era than ever before. The advent of social media and manufactured applications has rendered it much easier for individuals to generate income either by building their own lucrative brands or by working as freelancers in the gig economy. Not having work experience may preclude you from working for a traditional employer over more credential and experienced candidates, but will will not prevent you from being able to make money even if you lack transportation since most self-employed jobs can be fully completed remotely.

The advent of social media platforms has rendered it easier than ever before in the digital era for individuals to monetize their passions and hobbies. There are ample ways in which individuals can begin generating passive income. Platforms such as YouTube, Twitch, Patreon, Amazon Kindle, Blogger, Udemy, and Medium encourage creativity and allow content creators to parlay their passions and hobbies into lucrative opportunities for generating passive income streams. Being a content creator can truly be the utmost liberating and fulfilling job since it allows you to have full purview over your work, schedule, and business growth strategies. Monetizing your passions and hobbies can start with something as simple as producing videos and broadcasting live streams about your hobbies. Moreover, being a prolific content creator can eventually lend itself to other profitable passive income generating opportunities you would have never imagined possible as your brand grows and as you gain more clout as an influencer of your niche.

Earning substantially more than over 4 billion views per day, YouTube is the second largest search engine worldwide and provides a myriad of ways for content creators to capitalize on the opportunity to monetize their passions and hobbies. One of the primary ways to generate revenue on YouTube is through having advertisements run on your video content. When your channel has met the partnership criterion, you can being monetizing your video content with a Google AdSense account. This will enable you to begin generating passive income from your archived videos. To join the YouTube Partner Program, you will need to have earned at least 4,000 watch hours in the previous a year in addition to having a minimum of 1,000 subscribers. Additionally, Additionally, YouTubers can also sell product placements, avail themselves of sponsorship opportunities, can capitalize on affiliate marketing opportunities, can garner revenue from Super Chat donations, can receive royalty payments from selling customized brand merchandise, and can also generate revenue from selling channel memberships to earn more revenue.

The content creator can entice their followers to buy their customized brand merchandise sold through online stores, such as TeeSpring and CafePress, in order to draw forth royalty payments on product sales. These aforementioned companies not only produce the customized brand merchandise, but also do not mandate the content creator to be involved with any facets of the order fulfillment process.

Being apart of a sponsored campaign could entail something as simply as wearing a brand t-shirt on camera and redirecting viewers to the brand website through the content creator's affiliate link. Content creators can sleuth for sponsorship opportunities on websites such as, FameBit and Grapevine, to draw forth additional revenue streams.

The advantage of utilizing affiliate links is that they allow the content creator to generate commissions from product sales and do not require the content creator to succumb to dealing with any aspect of the order fulfillment process. Earning affiliate marketing revenue and royalties by referring prospective buyers to products can be purely profitable. Content creators for instance can enroll in affiliate programs and recommend for their viewers to buy products via their Amazon affiliate links (Stephenson, 2019) or eBay affiliate links to draw forth additional passive income streams.

The content creator can leverage their videos to provide recommendations of products, services, and websites. There are a myriad of ways to earn money though capitalizing on affiliate marketing opportunities since affiliate programs have a variety of payment options. Some affiliate programs pay per click (PPC) which means you can make money by redirecting your audience to the advertiser's website. On the other hand, other affiliate programs offer pay per lead (PPL) which entails earning money when your audience that has been redirected to the advertiser's website relinquishes their contact information on the advertiser's website. The most common payment option for affiliates is pay per sale (PPS) which culminates in affiliates earning revenue from commissions each time the advertiser generates sales from the affiliate's referrals.

Affiliate marketing opportunities can be highly profitable since you can organically recommend your audience to buy products and join websites without having to spend any money on advertising campaigns to redirect your traffic to an advertiser's website. Your constant creation of new content will help your brand organically build traction and allow you to attain clout as an influencer. You can capitalize on your clout by recommending products, services, and websites that you believe will provide value to your audience. The affiliate links can be embedded on your videos, live streams, and blogs posts.

Moreover, content creators can broadcast their hobbies on live streaming platforms, such as Twitch and Smashcast.TV. Twitch has become the YouTube of live streaming, allowing content creators to earn multiple streams of revenue, donations, and also gain significant exposure without having to overcome any barriers to entry to commence broadcasting their video footage. Popular Twitch streamers are generating substantially above the average household income per month as a result of having the power of clout and global digital distribution that they parlay into a profoundly lucrative career and business model. The release of the IRL category on Twitch has rendered it a platform for hobbyist and an online environment in which generating multiple streams of revenue for producing virtually any type of content is possible.

Moreover, there are a multitude of methods in which Twitch streamers can monetize their channels which encompass earning advertisement revenue, subscription revenue, sponsorship revenue, affiliate marketing revenue, and donations. Additionally, Twitch content creators also generate revenue from selling customized brand merchandise and from receiving bit cheers from their viewership. Streamers who do not have affiliate status nor partner status are barred from earning advertisement revenue, subscription revenue, and receiving bits from their viewership on Twitch.

Twitch subscription costs range from $4.99-$24.99 depending upon the monthly subscription price set forth by the live streamer. By subscribing to a streamer, viewers will have access to more emotes and access to a subscriber only chat. To supplement income, Twitch streamers utilize Patreon to procure monthly donations. Content creators will offer their patrons perks, such as the ability to vote for future content in a poll, in exchange for the gracious monthly donations from their patrons.

Beyond receiving the monthly subscription revenue and endless Patreon donation revenue, streamers also generation donation revenue through bits, Muxy, and Streamlabs. Bits are animated GIFs that viewers can utilize in chat which allows streamers to receive more revenue from Twitch each and every time their viewer cheer bits in the chat. Cheering bits can essentially be thought of as providing a donation to a streamer. Moreover, by submitting Streamlab donations, viewers can have access to text to speech donations or media sharing donations which allows them to influence the streamer's future content, especially as the streamer diverts away from their activities to address the requests and inquiries of their donors.

Similar to how Twitch streamers with affiliate or partner status can accept donation revenue from receiving bits, YouTube also allows streamers to accept donation revenue via super chat donations once they have met the criterion to enable super chat on their YouTube channel. As mentioned prior, being able to accept donations via Patreon, bit cheers, Super Chat, Muxy, Streamlabs, and PayPal, potentially from the entirety of your viewer base, can substantially add up overtime even if charitable contributions per individual donor are nominal.

Patreon donations can provide a consistent stream of monthly income for content creators. Content creators will offer their patrons perks, such as the ability to be access video content early, and will set reachable Patreon goals in exchange for the gracious monthly donations from their patrons. If enough people donate to the content creator then the Patreon goal will be reached and the content creator will subsequently produce special content to fulfill the goal, such as playing nostalgic retro video games that the patrons have yearned to watch the content creator attempt to complete.

The primarily reason donation revenue can be so lucrative for streamers, irrespective of the fact that there is no donation cap and viewers feel inclined to give back to content creators, is because viewers love being able to influence the streamer's content with their generous donations. For example, live streamer Ice Poseidon was able to earn over $5000 purely in an 8 hour period through donations by live streaming himself sleeping. Amid this live stream, viewers would keep submitting $100+ donations in an attempt to wake him up by having media sharing donations and text to speech donations play from Streamlabs. Donations are the currency to mold the streamer's future content, interact with the streamer, or elicit their thoughts about a particular topic.

Beyond setting up the virtual infrastructure to accept donations with links to Streamlabs and Muxy, the content who has attained affiliate or partner status on Twitch should ensure that pre-roll advertisements and mid-roll advertisements are being run so that they can reap advertisement revenue of around $2 per 1,000 impressions. Advertisement revenue can be exorbitant if the streamer has a substantial and growing audience. Content creators can capitalize on live streaming via Restream to multiple platforms simultaneously, such as YouTube, Twitch, and Smashcast.TV to accelerate brand growth, maximize audience reach, and optimize earnings potential. Ultimately, content creators that tap into the ample opportunities to generate revenue as a full time live streamer and can elicit a lucrative business model and career by passively generating far more revenue than they otherwise would earn by working a run of the mill 9 to 5 job.

Another option for individuals keen on monetizing their hobbies is to produce blogs, articles, and eBooks appertaining to their passions and hobbies. They can take advantage of the passive income generating opportunities that being a prolific author and building a blogging brand has to offer.

In the digital era, earning a substantial income as an author is now more viable than ever before. Authors can write about their hobbies and cherry pick shedding light on topics they are passionate about. Moreover, writers can generate revenue from multiple passive income sources beyond earning advertisement revenue from blog posts and beyond receiving royalty payments from eBook sales. Authors can parlay their clout and expertise into lucrative opportunities to further build their brand in a plethora of various ways, such as by creating automated courses and securing sponsorship deals. When devising a blogging brand and creating insightful blog posts, you want to offer so much merit in your content that brands that prospective readers cannot turn a blind eye towards reading your articles.

Generating revenue through being an author on Amazon Kindle Direct Publishing can be substantial overtime, especially for authors enrolled in KDP select. Enrolling in KDP select allows authors to reap a 70% royalty on eBook sales and also earn royalty payments commensurate with the number of Kindle Unlimited page read. Furthermore, prospective authors should focus on writing about niche topics and offering their eBooks for $3.99 or below to entice sales. Authors can also provide their books in both the hard-copy format and eBook format and can relinquish their eBooks for free as review copies. Having a higher sales volume will culminate in ranking higher in Amazon's search engine ranking algorithm which will lead to more sales overtime. Prolific authors can generate a livelihood solely through being published on Amazon since it is the number one platform for eBooks. Furthermore, they can also invest in leveraging Amazon advertisements to further amplify book sales.

In order to obtain more revenue, authors can enroll in Medium's Partner Program and can post articles called stories onto Medium. When Medium subscribers clap, the author receive a portion of their monthly subscription fee. The more frequently a Medium member claps, the smaller the portion the author receives of the individual Medium member's subscription fee. Therefore, Medium subscribers who clap the least frequently, allow authors to generate the utmost highest revenue from claps on their articles of up $1-$2 per clap whereas Medium subscribers who clap the most frequently only provide .01-.$1 per clap. Moreover, in terms of traffic, Medium is ranked in the top 300 most popular websites worldwide, and is ranked in the top 140 websites in the United States. Medium earns more than 60 million monthly readers and also allows blog imports (Blake, 2018) which renders it a lucrative platform for posts of insightful articles by prolific authors.

Authors can also capitalize on creating a blogger brand to draw forth advertisement revenue. Writers can earn advertisement revenue by generating this income per advertisement impression or per advertisement click on their blog. Advertisements can be embedded onto the sidebar, header, footer, and even in the text of their blog posts. Some of the myriad of popular advertisement networks that bloggers can join encompass Adsense, Sovrn, and Mediavine. These advertisement networks allow them to cherry pick the types of advertisements that the blogger wants to display on their blog. Even though CPMs and RPMs may be low as a result of a preponderance of readers enabling an AdBlocker extension in their browsers, one of the ways to compensate for this issue is to generate revenue from multiple passive income streams while creating a blog that offers so much merit that it is preordained to organically grow overtime to an unprecedented level. Some of the ample blogging platforms that can be utilize to commence blogging include Blogger, WordPress, and Jekyll.

Blogging can become an extremely lucrative pursuit overtime for prolific authors as their monetizable content reservoir of blogs continues to further expand and as the blogger's audience grows in size and support. By providing value upfront without asking for anything in return from the audience, the author can quickly earn the trust of their readership and likely begin monetizing their blog within a 6 month period. Authors should also understand the best search engine optimization (SEO) practices so that their content can be ranked high in Google's search engine.

In order to maximize readership levels overtime, writers should not only write about niche topics they are passionate about to maintain consistently posting daily blogging content, but should also select topics that have lasting power to write blogs about. Moreover, in order to establish a sizeable following, it will take a tremendous amount of time, dedication, and hard work on the writer's end. They will not only have to provide unprecedented value to their readership and understand best marketing practices to employ for building blog traction, but will need to create as much blog content as possible with lasting power to truly build up their passive income streams. They will also need to utilize social media platforms, such as Facebook and Twitter, to frequently promote their blogging brand and blog posts to further accelerate brand growth.

Another revenue stream writers can capitalize on growing is derived from creating paid sponsored posts. Writers that have a sizeable audience as influencers on blogs can secure sponsorship deals and subsequently create paid sponsored posts to promote a product or service. Sponsored networks specialize in providing job opportunities for bloggers with clout to secure deals with sponsoring brands. Writers can join a sponsored network, such as SoapBox Influence or the Pollinate network, to avail themselves of lucrative sponsored job opportunities to create paid sponsored content on behalf of other brands. To attain sponsorship revenue, authors will need to have a sizeable following and will need to have an audience that is apart of the sponsoring brand's target market.

Creating a blogging brand and consistently creating insightful blog content with lasting power can be a profitable income generating asset, especially as the continuous production of more meritorious blog content bolsters the brand growth, brand recognition, brand equity, and size of the blogging brand following. Creating a blogging brand is a viable strategy for earning multiple passive income streams overtime, monetizing your passion, and establishing yourself as an influencer. Blogging can also allow you to be perceived as an expert in your niche field and can pave the way for lucrative consulting opportunities in the future.

Another passive income stream content creators can generate is derived from selling automated online courses. Authors can utilize their blogging brand as a platform to entice readers to enroll in their automated online courses on educational websites, such as Udemy, Teachable, and Skillshare. Being able to set your own online course rates, earn commissions from the sales, and migrate your established following to an automated online course is an efficacious method for earning more passive income as a writer. The course content can be comprised of modules, videos, and articles. Moreover, you can also send subscribers of your email list a video pitching the course's merits and allow the self-led automated course to provide you with a consistent income stream if you have a sizeable following as a prolific author. The course should ideally provide enormous value and should offer content to your readership that cannot easily be accessed online.

A career as an author can be extremely lucrative in the long haul as a result of there being ample ways to generate passive income. Authors can earn passive income from eBook sales, Kindle Unlimited page reads, advertisement revenue, affiliate marketing revenue, Medium partner program revenue, and automated course enrollment revenue. Additionally, authors can also generate additional income streams from sponsorship revenue by creating paid sponsored posts and by also selling coaching packages (Moore, 2018). Growing a profitable blogging brand, producing an abundance of insightful articles daily, and producing a myriad of eBooks that establish yourself as an expert of niche can be extremely lucrative in the long haul as your following further grows and your content builds more traction overtime. Some of the utmost profitable passive streams that authors should focus on further growing encompass capitalizing on affiliate marketing opportunities, online course sales, and earn more revenue from Medium posts. With the power of digital global distribution, a career as an author is more viable than any other time in history for those who have the self-discipline, tenacity, expertise, and drive needed to actualize this dream to render it into a profitable, long lasting career.

Transforming your passion into a profitable career will involve providing a copious amount of meritorious content revolving around your niche, capitalizing on social media marketing to build more brand traction, and availing yourself of the ample passive income generating opportunities for monetizing your brand's contents. For instance, an artist can utilize Restream to simultaneously broadcast his live drawing sessions to YouTube, Smashcast.TV, and Twitch to grow a following and generate advertisements revenue. He can also utilize these channels to rally patron support and donations. Moreover, he can also produce eBook books and blogs appertaining to the best practices for how to produce all the various forms of art he is knowledgeable about. Once he has established substantial brand clout, he can secure sponsorship deals by selling product placement and also capitalize on affiliate marketing opportunities with links of products he recommends which can be embedded in his archived YouTube tutorial videos. The artist can also create automated online courses with exclusive insightful content about how to produce quality art and he can also sell his customized brand merchandise to reap royalty payments from followers of his brand.

Furthermore, the artist in this example can can capitalize on the utilizing IFTTT to create recipes to automate the dissemination of his social media marketing content. This is because, IFTTT is able to automatically disseminate the content creator's content, such as their YouTube video content, to a myriad of platforms simultaneously, such as Twitter, Pinterest, Tumblr, Blogger, and others social media outlets. The content creator can set the IFTTT recipes to trigger upon the condition of new videos being uploaded to YouTube. By automating content marketing practices and social media marketing practices by leveraging IFTTT recipes, content creators can focus on spending far time producing content and less time marketing content.

The most efficacious strategy for marketing your brand in the digital era involves automating as many marketing processes and marketing activities as possible. As mentioned previously, this can be achieved through establishing as many recipes as possible by utilizing IFTTT to automatically disseminate your content to as many social media platforms as possible, such as Twitter, Pinterest, Tumblr and other outlets whenever you produce new content.

Moreover, to further accelerate brand growth, the content creator can invest in utilizing Facebook advertisements, Adwords campaigns, and social media influencers to entice more viewers to watch their brand's content. The new viewers may become the content creator's future customers, patrons, and brand ambassadors. Digital marketing campaigns can be an efficacious usage of marketing dollars since they provide brands with access to analytical data that they can meticulously analyze to learn how to easily refine marketing campaigns and more prudently spend marketing dollars going forward.

It is more viable than anytime in history to monetize your passions and hobbies and covert into a profitable full time career online. Transforming your passion into a profitable career will not only involve providing a copious amount of meritorious content revolving around your niche, capitalizing on social media marketing to build more brand traction, and availing yourself of the ample passive income generating opportunities for monetizing your brand's contents, but will allow require unwavering commitment, hard work, dedication, and an exorbitant amount of time. Sharing your passions and hobbies on social media platforms can potentially provide you with a substantially higher income stream in the long haul than you would otherwise earn lumbering your way up the corporate hierarchy. Selling your time for money caps your earnings potential, whereas the power of global digital distribution not only allows you to reach out to over 8 billion people and monetize your intellectual properties and intellectual capital, but can also offer content creators a limitless earnings potential.

Beyond the aforementioned job opportunities, individuals that are more inclined to pursue freelance work instead of earmarking their time into building their own brands can utilize manufactured application such as Rover, Lift, Uber Eats, Door Dash, Task Rabbit, and Gig Walker (Blake, 2018) to find immediate job opportunities. These aforementioned applications, not only allows individuals to avail themselves of job opportunities they can cherry pick, but also allow them to find work at any given time that coincides with their busy schedules. Young adults in the digital era have an easier time finding temporary jobs than their predecessor generations had since manufactured applications can now connect individuals looking for work to clients in an eminently expeditious manner.

Individuals are utilizing applications to avail themselves of rudimentary job opportunities that entail jobs such as delivering packaging, driving around passengers, walking dogs, moving furniture, completing odd jobs, writing reviews, completing handyman work, providing house keeping services, and undergoing lawn mowing services. Although these job opportunities may be short lived, potentially allowing you to complete over ten jobs in a day if you hustle, individuals have plenty of opportunities to find work instantaneously through the usage of manufactured applications since new job openings are abundant and clients utilizing these applications are not selective who they hire as long the worker has the competent and skill sets need to complete these mostly rudimentary jobs.

Moreover, individuals looking for longer term work opportunities can submit proposals on freelancer websites, such as Fiverr and Upwork, to secure more remote, computer based work, such as editing videos, writing research articles, managing marketing campaigns, and creating graphic designs. Payments from these longer term entrepreneurial pursuits through freelancer websites may only be receivable post the project being completed.

The gig economy is becoming the new paradigm of the job market. By utilizing independent contracts instead of full time employee, companies can minimize their labor costs, can mitigate hiring risks, and can minimize their liabilities. Moreover, they do not have to pay their independent contractor workforce benefits nor salaries. This business model allows companies to offer services for reduced costs on the customer's end since they do not have incur all the labor costs associated with having a full time workforce. Moreover, individuals love the flexibility of being able to be self-employed and work on their own terms. By working these temporary jobs in the gig economy for supplementary income, individuals are not bound to adhering to a stringent schedule nor are obligated into fulfilling long term commitment.

Furthermore, the ability to cherry pick the work on demand jobs without undergoing the hassle and tedium of having to submit any applications after the individual laborer has already been signed up for the applications truly renders these job enticing opportunities for all parities to capitalize on since everyone benefits, even if the pay is low on the independent contractor's end. These jobs opportunities have little to no barriers to entry, are simplistic to complete, and can be procured on demand.

The gig economy jobs also provide the inexperienced labor force participants the opportunity to gain work experience and dabble into working in different fields until they find the jobs they are most content with fulfilling going forward. With millions of workers rapidly entering the gig economy, it is highly likely that it will begin to become the primary job market of the future as employers and clients seek cheaper labor with minimal risks on both of their ends. The companies that connect clients with independent contracts can act as a mediator if an issue arises during the job even if they are more than likely inclined to side with their client over their independent contractors. This is because, they may be more concerned with retaining the clients' business and may deem their independent contractors to be an expendable and easily replaceable workforce, especially if their clients are dissatisfied with the outcome of the services performed.

In conclusion, being able to secure temporary employment on a daily basis is easier than ever before in the digital era in part due to advent of freelancer websites and the proliferation of manufactured applications that offer ample gig economy jobs on demand for inexperienced workers. Moreover, individuals can also start parlaying their talents, skills, and knowledge into growing a lucrative niche brand that can provide them with ample streams of passive income. The revenue generating opportunities global distribution platforms provide content creators are unprecedented since they allow content creators to reach out to potentially over 8 billion viewers that may feel inclined to support the content creator if they deem their content to be appealing and meritorious. Ultimately, with online platforms such as YouTube, Twitch, Patreon, Amazon Kindle, Blogger, Udemy, and Medium with no barriers to entry which allow anyone to produce content online, and with the ubiquity of applications that provide on-demand work, individuals at any level should be able to easily attain work at any time with minimal job search effort on their ends.

It is significantly easier today than anytime in history for rising influencers to earn revenue online and take control of their lives as they are in the nascent stages of building their brands as content creators. Being able to earn enough revenue online to be able to afford to focus solely on being a full time influencer and content creator without ever needing to succumb to working for an employer is more viable than anytime in history. Fortunately, retiring amid their early adulthood years and becoming wealthy is more viable than ever before for those who are able to attain extreme fame leverage and profound success online as a world renowned influencer. An influencer with extreme fame leverage can easily earn more money in one day than the average person will earn working multiple jobs throughout the entirety of their lifetime. Influencers who have attained extreme fame leverage are easily able to take control of their work lives, eminently enrich every aspect of their lives, and create the lives they always envisioned.

# References

*5 Benefits of Being an Influencer.* (2018).

    Retrieved from

        http://blog.shopandshout.com/5-benefits-of-being-an-influencer

Badenhausen, K. (2019). The Highest-Paid Tennis Players 2019: Roger Federer

    Scores A Record $93 Million. Retrieved from

    https://forbes.com/sites/kurtbadenhausen/2019/08/26/highest-paid-tennis-players-roger-federer/#3a80b2d46cc6/

*Become a Jewelry Maker: Education and Career Roadmap.* (2019).

    Retrieved from

    https://study.com/articles/Become_a_Jewelry_Maker_Education_and_Career_Roadmap.html

Blake, T. (2018). How To Make Money on Medium - My First Medium Paycheck.

    Retrieved from

        https://thisonlineworld.com/2018/04/06/medium-writing/

Blake, T. (2018). The Best Gig Economy Jobs – Make Extra Money On The

    Side. Retrieved from

    https://thisonlineworld.com/2018/08/25/gig-economy/

Cohn, M. (n.d.). The Effectiveness of Networking Through Meetup.

    Retrieved from

    https://www.compukol.com/the-effectiveness-of-networking-through-meetup/

Csiszar, M. (2017). How to Become a Successful Stockbroker.

    Retrieved from

        https://careertrend.com/average-monthly-income-stock-broker-7755.html

Franek, T. (n.d.). 5 Benefits of Taking AP Classes in High School.

    Retrieved from

        https://www.princetonreview.com/college-advice/ap-classes

*How do I start a Meetup group?* (n.d.).

    Retrieved from

        https://help.meetup.com/hc/en-us/articles/360002882111-How-do-I-start-a-Meetup-group-

Moore, A. (2018). The Best 4 Ways To Earn Income Writing in 2018 (and the 3 Worst). \

    Retrieved from https://medium.com/the-mission/the-4-best-ways-to-earn-income-writing-in-2018-and-the-3-worst-16b486c19774

Moskowitz, A. (2019). How to Become a Successful Stockbroker.

    Retrieved from

        https://www.investopedia.com/articles/professionals/051915/how-become-successful-stock-broker.asp

Nanor, D. (2018). 6 High Income Skills Anyone Can Learn To Become Financially Free.

    Retrieved from

        https://hellogiggles.com/news/kylie-jenner-instagram-post-million/

O'Kane, C. (2018). Top 10 highest-paid YouTube stars of 2018, according to Forbes.

    Retrieved from

https://www.tlnt.com/the-top-10-reasons-why-networking-events-are-a-waste-of-a-jobseekers-time/

Prater, M. (2019). 15 Trusted Ways to Generate Seller Leads in Real Estate. Retrieved from

https://blog.hubspot.com/sales/real-estate-leads

Sienkiewicz, T. (2019). Top 5 Things to Know About DSST and CLEP Exams and Full List of Exams Offered. Retrieved from

https://www.petersons.com/blog/top-5-things-to-know-about-dsst-and-clep-exams-and-list-of-dsst-and-clep-exams-offered/

Spencer, B. (2014). Meetup.com: A Secret Weapon for Your Career and Personal Brand. Retrieved from

https://www.huffpost.com/entry/using-meetupcom-as-a-bran_b_4767898

Stephenson, B. (2019, March 29). How Gamers Are Making a Full-Time Living Playing Video Games on Twitch. Retrieved from

https://www.lifewire.com/make-money-streaming-on-twitch-4144817

Sullivan, J. (2018). The Top 10 Reasons Why Networking Events Are a Waste of a Jobseeker's Time. Retrieved from

https://www.tlnt.com/the-top-10-reasons-why-networking-events-are-a-waste-of- a-jobseekers-time/

Payne, K. (n.d.). How to Become an Influencer in Your Industry. Retrieved from

https://blog.hubspot.com/marketing/how-to-become-an-influencer-in-10-steps

Petersen, L. (2019). What Is the Percent of Profit Margin That Retailers Expect From Jewelry?.

    Retrieved from

    https://smallbusiness.chron.com/percent-profit-margin-retailers-expect-jewelry-73996.html

Totka, M. (2017). *6 Ways to Save Your Small Business from Closing.*

    Retrieved from

    https://www.business.com/articles/megan-totka-save-business-from-closing/

Vanderberg, M. (2018). We just found out how much Kylie Jenner makes per Instagram post, and our college degrees feel useless.

    Retrieved from

    https://hellogiggles.com/news/kylie-jenner-instagram-post-million/

Weisbrot, E. (2018). Step-by-Step Guide: How to Become a contractor.

    Retrieved from

    https://www.jwsuretybonds.com/blog/step-by-step-guide-how-to-become-a-contractor

## Disclaimer

"The author assumes absolutely no responsibility for anyone's actions, choices, nor results under any circumstance". The reader assumes full responsibility for their actions, choices, and results. The author does not guarantee any results under any circumstance. This book is not intended as a substitute for the "financial advice of financial professionals. You should never make any financial decision without first consulting with your own financial adviser and conducting your own research and due diligence".

331.25729 SAC
**Sachs, Harrison**
**How to earn money**
 **immediately in the Gig**

07/19/21

CPSIA information can be obtained
at www.ICGtesting.com
Printed in the USA
LVHW011503050721
691876LV00008B/1021